east &
south-east

east &
south-east

great recipes from china, japan and south-east asia

Sonia Stevenson, Clare Ferguson,
Fiona Smith and Elsa Petersen-Schepelern

RYLAND
PETERS
& SMALL

LONDON NEW YORK

Senior Designer Steve Painter

Editors Elsa Petersen-Schepelern, Kathy Steer

Production Deborah Wehner

Art Director Gabriella Le Grazie

Publishing Director Alison Starling

Indexer Hilary Bird

First published in Great Britain in 2002
by Ryland Peters & Small
Kirkman House, 12–14 Whitfield Street,
London W1T 2RP
www.rylandpeters.com

10 9 8 7 6 5 4 3 2 1

Recipes in this book have previously been published in
other Ryland Peters & Small books (see page 144).

ISBN 1 84172 336 3

A catalogue record for this book is available from the
British Library

Printed in China

Notes

•All spoon measurements are level.

•All eggs are large, unless otherwise specified.
Uncooked or partly cooked eggs should not be served
to the very young, the very old, those with compromised
immune systems, or to pregnant women.

•To sterilize preserving jars, wash the jars in hot, soapy
water and rinse in boiling water. Put in a large saucepan
and pour over enough water to cover. With the lid on,
bring the water to the boil and continue boiling for
15 minutes. Turn off the heat and leave the jars in the
water until they are to be filled. Invert the jars onto clean
kitchen paper to dry. Sterilize the lids for 5 minutes by
boiling. Jars should be filled and sealed while still hot.

•East and South-east Asian ingredients are available in
Asian markets, Chinese, Japanese and South-east Asian
shops. A limited range of ingredients is sold in some
wholefood shops, larger supermarkets, kitchen shops
and delicatessens.

contents

east & south-east ...

Everyone loves Chinese food – from easy takeaways in pretty boxes, to a trip to a restaurant with the kids to play with chopsticks, to cooking it yourself (anyone can do stir-fry). However, these days we're falling in love with other kinds of Asian food too – Japanese sushi, Korean grills, Thai curries, Vietnamese spring rolls – and even lesser known cuisines like Indonesian, Cambodian and Malaysian. All delicious, and much easier to cook than you might think. This book is an introduction to recipes from East and South-east Asia, but you'll need a few special items first ...

Special Ingredients

Many Asian ingredients are now found in supermarkets. Think soy sauce. Think Asian herbs such as coriander and mint, or ready-made Thai spice pastes, or stir-fry vegetables, now even chopped for you and sealed in convenient plastic bags.

However, some other ingredients are only just finding their way into the mainstream and you may need to make a special visit to a Chinese grocer or an Asian market, or order from a specialist website. There you'll find a fascinating experience for any cook. You might go just to buy a few dried mushrooms for a recipe, but then end up with a huge bag groaning with three kinds of noodles, rice from Vietnam, ketjap manis (sweet soy sauce) from Indonesia, barbecued duck, the freshest fish and seafood, Japanese yuzu juice, star anise in kilo bags, Chinese yard-long beans, pea shoots, Thai kaffir lime leaves, lemongrass and more.

Luckily most of these wonderful ingredients, especially the flavourings, can be frozen. However, if you can't find them, don't panic. Either substitute something similar – lime zest instead of kaffir lime leaves, lemon zest instead of lemongrass, or soy sauce instead of fish sauce. Or just leave them out. The dish will taste or look slightly different, but local cooks would do the same.

Special equipment

The good thing is that Asian food very easy to make. Remember that, until recently, people in the region cooked very simply over an open fire. This means that their cooking utensils are sturdy and simple, so with our stainless steel saucepan sets, five-burner cook tops, barbecues and fan-assisted ovens, we should be ready for anything.

So what do you need to start? Of course, you can use your existing utensils, but who, these days, would be without a wok? There are all kinds and all sizes – even flat-bottomed woks for use on electric stove tops. Many cooks prefer the simple, inexpensive iron kind sold in Chinatown. When you buy them, they're covered with a light film of machine oil

applied at the factory. You should scrub it off with a scouring detergent, rinse well, then dry. Heat 2 tablespoons or so of tasteless vegetable oil in the wok – corn or peanut are perfect. Rub it all over the inside of the wok with kitchen paper, then put the wok over low heat and leave it there for 20 minutes. Pour out the oil and rub all over with kitchen paper until the paper is clean. The wok should never be washed in soap again, but only wiped clean with kitchen paper while still hot, or rinsed in hot water. Dry well and rub with a little oil if you're not going to use it straight away. You'll soon end up with a perfect, black, virtually non-stick surface. Store the wok upside down, so moisture doesn't collect in the bottom and make it rusty. If it does, it's not the end of the world. Just scour it clean, rinse well, rub with oil and heat as before.

A steamer will be incredibly useful. Perhaps your saucepan set has a steamer insert, but many don't, so go to Chinatown and start a collection of beautiful (inexpensive) bamboo steamers (also available from many regular kitchen shops). But even if you haven't got one of these, you can put a plate upside down in a regular saucepan, put another plate on top of that and steam the food on the plate.

And chopsticks. They're some of the best cooking implements ever invented; they stir, they beat, they turn, they fry. Beginners get into a terrible tizz about how to hold them. Simple – just don't think about it. After a few minutes, especially using them for cooking, the knack will come naturally. (Incidentally – a bit of chopstick good manners; don't put the end you put in your mouth into a communal dish. Turn them round and pick up food from a serving dish with the back end of the chopsticks.)

Try the recipes in *East & South-east*. They range from the quick and simple to some challenging dishes for experienced cooks. Try new ingredients whenever you find them, and if you find you just adore one or more of these cuisines – say Vietnamese, or Japanese, or Korean – you'll know which restaurant to try next time! It's a good way to learn.

snacks &streetfood

Streetfood in East and South-east Asia is legendary, full of colour and flavour, and varied enough for anyone's taste. Make these dishes as snacks, serve them as starters, hand them round as party canapés – your guests will love them.

vietnamese pork balls
with chilli dipping sauce

500 g pork mince

6 garlic cloves, crushed

2 stalks of lemongrass, trimmed and finely sliced

a bunch of coriander, finely chopped

2 fresh red chillies, deseeded and chopped

1 tablespoon brown sugar

1 tablespoon Vietnamese or Thai fish sauce

1 egg, beaten

salt and freshly ground black pepper

peanut oil, for frying

Chilli dipping sauce

125 ml white rice vinegar

2–6 small or 1 large fresh red chilli, finely sliced

1 tablespoon Vietnamese or Thai fish sauce

1 spring onion, finely sliced (optional)

½–1 tablespoon brown sugar

Makes about 12

A delicious traditional recipe that's perfect for a drinks party. The original is manna from heaven to the dedicated chilli-head. Don't just up the chilli because you love it – remember some people don't. And of course your guests will drink more to cool the fires, never realizing that water or alcohol won't help soothe a chilli burn (only milk or yoghurt will, in case you're interested!) Use fat Fresno chillies for a mild flavour, or tiny bird's eye chillies for blinding heat. Fish sauce is used as a seasoning in Vietnamese cooking – like salt or soy sauce. If you can't find it, use salt instead (not as interesting, but OK at a pinch.)

Put all the ingredients for the chilli dipping sauce into a small bowl and stir thoroughly to dissolve the sugar. Cover and set aside to develop the flavours.

To make the pork balls, put all the remaining ingredients except the peanut oil into a large bowl and mix well. Dip your hands in water, take about 1–2 tablespoons of the mixture, and roll it into a ball. Repeat with the remaining mixture. Put the balls, spaced well apart, onto a plate as you finish them. Chill in the refrigerator for at least 30 minutes.

Fill a wok one-third full of peanut oil and heat to 190°C (375°F), or until a piece of noodle puffs up immediately. Add the pork balls, 6 at a time, and deep-fry in batches until golden brown. Remove with a slotted spoon and drain on crumpled kitchen paper, keeping them warm in the oven until all the balls are cooked. Serve with the chilli dipping sauce.

thai crabcakes
with chilli dipping sauce

Everyone loves Thai fishcakes and crabcakes. Chopped green beans or chopped asparagus are popular additions with Western chefs, but snake beans (Chinese yard-long beans) have a better texture as well as a more interesting taste. Use ordinary beans if you can't find them.

3 fresh red chillies, deseeded

3 spring onions, finely sliced

2 garlic cloves, crushed

4 stalks of coriander, finely chopped

3 cm fresh ginger or galangal, chopped

6 fresh kaffir lime leaves, finely sliced, or grated zest of 2 limes

1 tablespoon Vietnamese or Thai fish sauce

250 g boneless fish fillets, such as cod

250 g crabmeat (fresh, frozen or canned)

2 snake beans (Chinese yard-long beans), finely sliced

30 g beanthread (cellophane) noodles (1 small bundle)

1 egg, beaten

2 tablespoons peanut oil

Chilli dipping sauce

125 ml white rice vinegar

1 fresh red chilli, finely sliced

1 tablespoon Vietnamese or Thai fish sauce

1 spring onion, finely sliced

1 teaspoon brown sugar

Makes about 30

Put the chillies, spring onions, garlic, coriander stalks, ginger or galangal, kaffir lime leaves or lime zest, and fish sauce into a food processor and process to a paste. Add the fish and continue to process until smooth. Transfer to a bowl and mix in the crabmeat and snake beans.

Put the beanthread noodles into a bowl and cover with hot water. Let soak for 5 minutes, then drain and, using a pair of scissors, snip into short pieces, about 3 cm long. Mix into the fish mixture and stir in the beaten egg. Wet your hands with water and shape the mixture into flat hamburger-shaped patties of about 1–2 tablespoons each.

Heat the peanut oil in a wok or frying pan and swirl to coat the sides. Add the crabcakes, 3 at a time, and fry until golden. Transfer to a plate lined with kitchen paper and keep hot in the oven while you cook the remaining crabcakes.*

Put all the dipping sauce ingredients into a small bowl and stir well. Serve with the crabcakes.

*Note For a crisper finish, the crabcakes can also be sprinkled with rice flour before cooking, then deep-fried.

Meat and rice wrapped in Chinese leaves make perfect dim sum (little Chinese snacks). There are many popular vegetables from the cabbage family in Chinese cuisine – any, as long as the leaves are big enough, are suitable here.

bok choy rolls with spicy chicken

100 g (125 ml) long grain rice

36 large Chinese leaves, such as large bok choy, pak choy or Chinese cabbage, about 500 g

350 g skinless, boneless chicken breast, minced

6 spring onions, chopped

2 garlic cloves, crushed

4 cm fresh ginger, peeled and grated

2 fresh green chillies, deseeded and finely chopped

2 teaspoons Chinese five-spice powder

2 tablespoons hoisin or yellow bean sauce

150 g canned water chestnuts, drained and chopped

Plum Sauce (page 37), to serve

a bamboo steamer

Makes 36

Bring a large saucepan of lightly salted water to the boil. Add the rice and cook for 10 minutes. Drain thoroughly.

Separate the leaves of the bok choy – each should be at least 12 x 8 cm. Bring a separate saucepan of water to the boil, add the leaves and blanch for a few minutes. Refresh in cold water.

Put the chicken, spring onions, garlic, ginger, chillies, Chinese five-spice powder, hoisin or yellow bean sauce and water chestnuts into a bowl and mix well.

Put 1 tablespoon of the mixture into the centre of each leaf and roll up, then put into a steamer set over a pan of boiling water and steam for 10 minutes. Serve with plum sauce.

vietnamese spring rolls
with pickles and dipping sauce

Vietnam has produced one of the world's truly great cuisines – fresh with salads and herbs, and less oily than Chinese food. This recipe includes two of its greatest components – pickles and a dipping sauce.

60 g beanthread (cellophane) noodles (2 bundles)*

1 packet Vietnamese ricepaper wrappers (*bahn trang*)**

1 butterhead lettuce, leaves finely shredded

leaves from a large bunch of fresh Vietnamese herbs, such as coriander and mint

Chinese barbecued pork, duck or prawns, finely sliced or shredded

Pickled carrots and radishes

1–2 carrots

about 10 radishes

2 teaspoons rice vinegar

2 pinches of salt

4 teaspoons sugar

Nuóc cham dipping sauce

1 garlic clove, crushed

½ hot fresh red chilli, finely chopped

1 tablespoon sugar

juice from 1 wedge of lime

2 tablespoons Vietnamese or Thai fish sauce

Serves 4

*See note page 47

**Ricepaper wrappers are sold in packages of 50 or 100. Seal leftovers in the same package, put into a plastic bag and seal well.*

To make the pickles, peel the carrots and cut into long, thin strips with a vegetable peeler. Alternatively, slice on a mandoline. Roll up and cut into very thin strips. Finely slice the radishes on a mandoline or with a sharp knife – aim for see-through slices. Put the carrot strips into 1 bowl and the radishes into another. Divide the vinegar, salt and sugar between the bowls, then add 125 ml water to each one. Set aside for at least 15 minutes or up to 24 hours. Drain before using.

To make the dipping sauce, grind the garlic, chilli and sugar to a paste with a mortar and pestle. Add the lime juice, fish sauce and 2½ tablespoons of water.

Put the noodles into a bowl and cover with hot water. Let soak for 15 minutes, then drain and keep in cold water until ready to serve.

To prepare the spring rolls, dip 1 ricepaper sheet into a large dish of water for about 30 seconds until softened. Transfer to a plate (not a board, or they will dry out). On one side of the sheet, put a few shreds of lettuce, noodles, herbs, pork, duck or prawn, and a pickled carrot and radish. There should be lots of herbs.

Roll up the ricepaper like a cigar and repeat until all the ingredients have been used. Put the rolls onto a serving platter, spray with a mist of water and cover with a damp cloth or kitchen paper until ready to serve. To serve, spray with water again and serve with the dipping sauce. Alternatively, serve the ingredients on separate plates for guests to assemble their own rolls.

Note If Chinese barbecued duck is unavailable, rub 2 duck breasts with Chinese five-spice powder and marinate in the refrigerator for 15 minutes. Transfer to a preheated frying pan, skin side down, and cook for 10 minutes or until the skin is crisp, the fat runs and the flesh is cooked half through. Turn them over and cook the other side until medium rare. Set aside, let cool, then slice finely.

Barbecuing is one of the most typical Korean cooking methods. On Sundays, all over Seoul – indeed over much of Korea – you'll see families at outdoor restaurants serving bulgogi and *kalbi chim* (glazed char-grilled spareribs), the two favourite local street foods.

Bulgogi is finely sliced marinated beef, briefly flashed on both sides over a preheated metal surface. Crisp leaves are filled with the beef, fruit and kimchee, Korea's famous chilli-powered pickle, then rolled up and eaten with the fingers.

bulgogi
korean barbecued beef

1.5 kg beef fillet, finely sliced*

Barbecue marinade
125 ml dark soy sauce
60 g caster sugar
3 garlic cloves, finely chopped
4 spring onions, finely chopped
3 cm fresh ginger, peeled and grated
2 tablespoons sesame oil
2 tablespoons toasted sesame seeds

To serve
30 crisp lettuce leaves
175 g canned kimchee pickle (Korean cabbage)
2 Asian pears (*nashi*), crisp apples or nectarines, cut into wedges
8 spring onions, cut into strips lengthways
2 tablespoons toasted sesame seeds

a bulgogi pan, stove-top grill pan or frying pan

Serves 6

Put all the marinade ingredients into a large, shallow bowl, add the beef slices and turn until well coated. Cover and chill in the refrigerator for 30 minutes.

Assemble all the serving accompaniments in separate bowls before cooking.

Heat a bulgogi pan, stove-top grill pan or frying pan until very hot. Using tongs, add the beef slices, one at a time. Let cook until aromatic, then turn and cook the other side. (The outside should be caramelized and the insides succulent and tender, but cook it longer if you prefer.)

Each person takes a lettuce leaf, adds a piece of beef, quartered, if necessary, and their choice of kimchee, pears, spring onions and sesame seeds.

***Note** To make the beef easier to slice, freeze it first for about 1 hour. Slice when frozen – it will have thawed by the time you want to cook it.

Sui mai, the Chinese name for these dumplings, means 'cook and eat'. They are one of the most famous dim sum or streetfoods and make perfect party food. Cook in bamboo steamers, three layers at a time, and serve that batch, still in the steamers, while you cook the next. Make them with pork or chicken – both are delicious.

chinese dim sum
steamed dumplings

425 g minced pork or chicken

125 g shelled prawns

3 slices smoked streaky bacon, chopped

1 teaspoon crushed Szechuan pepper or freshly ground black pepper

1 egg white

2 teaspoons sesame oil

3 cm fresh ginger, peeled and grated

2 teaspoons salt

2 fat garlic cloves, crushed

2 teaspoons cornflour

4 spring onions

4 canned water chestnuts, finely chopped

4 snake beans (Chinese yard-long beans) or 10 green beans, finely sliced

1–2 packets wonton wrappers*

flour, for dusting

soy sauce or chilli sauce, to serve

several bamboo steamers lined with banana leaves or baking parchment

Serves 10

*Packets vary, but contain about 40 large (10 cm) or 70 small (8 cm) wrappers. Leftover wrappers can be frozen.

Put the pork or chicken, prawns and bacon into a food processor and process until smooth. With the motor running, add the pepper, egg white, sesame oil, ginger, salt, garlic and cornflour.

Using a sharp knife, finely chop the white and green parts of the spring onions crossways, then transfer to a large mixing bowl. Add the pork mixture, water chestnuts and beans and mix well.

Take the wonton wrappers out of the plastic bag, but keep any you are not using covered with plastic as you work, because they dry out quickly.

Using a pair of scissors, cut the square wonton wrappers into rounds, then put 1 tablespoon of the filling into the centre of each one. Use a small spatula to smooth the mixture almost to the edges.

Cup the wonton in your hand. Bring your fingers together to achieve an open-topped, pleated, bag-shaped container – press the filling down gently with a spatula as you do so. Drop the dumpling gently onto a lightly floured surface to flatten the base and settle the filling. Repeat until all the dumplings are made.

Set the dumplings on several racks of a bamboo steamer lined with banana leaves or baking parchment. Fill a wok about one-third full of water and bring to the boil. Put the steamers into the wok, cover and steam for 7–10 minutes, refilling the base with boiling water as necessary. Serve hot with a simple dip of soy sauce or chilli sauce.

chopstick chicken wontons

Many versions of wontons and wonton soup are found all over China. Making and shaping the wontons takes less time than you'd think – the main thing is to ensure a tight, effective seal. Buy wonton wrappers in bulk, wrap them in packs of 40 and freeze for future use: they thaw quickly and well. You can then make wontons easily – on a whim.

2 litres chicken stock, preferably homemade

4 spring onions, sliced into long strips

1 packet wonton wrappers, about 36*

Wonton filling

350 g uncooked chicken breast, minced

5 cm fresh ginger, peeled and grated

2 fresh red chillies, deseeded and chopped

1 egg

2 tablespoons sesame oil, preferably unrefined

2 teaspoons sea salt flakes

1 teaspoon freshly ground black pepper

To serve

4 tablespoons sesame seeds, pan-toasted (optional)

dipping sauces such as soy, chilli or yellow bean sauce

Serves 4; makes 36

*Packets vary, but contain about 40 large (10 cm) or 70 small (8 cm) wrappers. Leftover wrappers can be frozen.

Put the chicken stock and spring onions into a large, wide saucepan and bring to the boil. Reduce to a simmer and cover with a lid.

To make the wonton filling, put the minced chicken, ginger, chillies, egg, sesame oil, salt and pepper into a bowl and mix well.

Take the wonton wrappers out of the plastic bag, but keep them covered with plastic as you work, because they dry out quickly.

Put the wonton wrappers onto the work surface and put 1 heaped teaspoon of the mixture into the centre of each one. Wet the edges with water and fold one half over the other to form a triangle, pinching the edges together. Wet the 2 folded points and pinch them together to seal, making them into a circle. Continue until all the filling has been used (freeze any leftover wrappers). Don't let the wontons touch each other or they may stick together.

Return the stock to a rolling boil and add the wontons to the saucepan all at once. Cook for 4 minutes, then, when they have risen to the surface, remove with a slotted spoon. Serve in little china bowls, sprinkled with toasted sesame seeds, if using, and with some of the dipping sauce spooned over. Serve extra dipping sauce separately. Eat with chopsticks.

Wontons are easy to make and you can vary the fillings, using prawns, crabmeat or chicken. They make spectacular party food – serve them with a simple soy sauce dip or a chilli dip for your spice-loving friends!

chinese crispy deep-fried wontons

125 g minced pork

4 garlic cloves, crushed

4 water chestnuts or 2 bamboo shoots, chopped

1–2 packets wonton wrappers*

1 egg, beaten

a bunch of fresh Chinese chives, blanched in boiling water (optional)

salt and freshly ground black pepper

peanut oil, for frying

soy sauce, to serve (optional)

Dipping sauce (optional)

1 tablespoon soy sauce

1 fresh red chilli, sliced

1 spring onion, finely sliced

1 tablespoon rice vinegar

Serves 4

*Packets vary, but contain about 40 large (10 cm) or 70 small (8 cm) wrappers. Leftover wrappers can be frozen.

Put the minced pork into a food processor with the garlic, salt and pepper and process until smooth. Transfer to a bowl and mix in the chopped water chestnuts or bamboo shoots.

Put all the dipping sauce ingredients into a small bowl and mix well. Put onto a large serving platter and set aside until required.

Take the wonton wrappers out of the plastic bag, but keep any you are not using covered with plastic as you work, because they dry out quickly.

Put 1 wonton wrapper onto the work surface and put 1 tablespoon of filling into the centre. Brush a circle of beaten egg around the filling, pull up the sides of the wonton wrapper and twirl the free part of the pastry close up against the ball of filling, so you have a frilly top. Open out the frill. You can tie a blanched chive around the join if you like, but the egg acts as glue.

When all the wontons are assembled, fill a wok one-third full of peanut oil and heat to 190°C (375°F), or until a piece of noodle puffs up immediately.

Add the wontons, 3–4 at a time, and deep-fry for a few minutes on each side until brown and crisp. Do not let the oil get too hot, or the wonton pastry will cook before the filling.

Using a slotted spoon, transfer to a plate covered with crumpled kitchen paper to drain. Keep them warm in a low oven while you cook the remaining wontons (use a slotted spoon to skim any debris from the oil between batches).

Serve hot, with the dipping sauce and a small dish of plain soy sauce, if using, for the less fiery personalities among your guests!

indonesian chicken martabak

250 g cooked, boneless chicken (breast or thigh), cut into 1 cm pieces

1–2 teaspoons Malay-style hot curry paste

2 tablespoons mango chutney

3 cm fresh ginger, peeled and grated

1 stalk of lemongrass, trimmed and very finely sliced (optional)

about 8 large sprigs of coriander or mint leaves, sliced

1 packet wonton wrappers*

1 egg white

peanut oil, for frying

Dipping sauces

125 ml sweet chilli sauce

125 ml Indonesian soy sauce (*ketjap manis*) or regular soy sauce

a large heavy-based saucepan

Serves 4; makes 20

Packets vary, but contain about 40 large (10 cm) or 70 small (8 cm) wrappers. Leftover wrappers can be frozen.

This culturally hybrid, ravioli-type recipe contains ready-cooked chicken, such as leftover poached or roasted chicken. Malay curry paste, Indian-style mango chutney and Chinese wonton wrappers complete the picture. The filling, though unorthodox, is delicious.

Fresh wonton wrappers from specialist Asian food shops can be purchased in bulk, then packaged in, say, lots of 40, and frozen. They take 30 minutes to 1 hour to thaw, and are useful for many recipes.

Put the chicken, curry paste, chutney, ginger, lemongrass, if using, and coriander or mint into a food processor and process in brief bursts until coarsely chopped. Transfer to a small bowl and set aside.

Take the wonton wrappers out of the plastic bag, but keep any you are not using covered with plastic as you work, because they dry out quickly.

Working with 8 wonton wrappers at a time, put them onto a work surface and paint a border of egg white around the edge of 4. Set 1 level teaspoon of filling into the centre of each one. Cover with a second wrapper and, using the sides of your hands, press down to seal the edges. Repeat to make 20 parcels in all.

Fill a heavy-based saucepan to a 7.5 cm depth with peanut oil and heat to 190°C (375°F), or until a piece of noodle puffs up immediately. Add the wonton parcels in batches of 4 and cook for 6–8 seconds, pushing them down under the bubbling oil. Using tongs, turn them over carefully and cook the other side for 6 seconds. As they cook, they expand, crinkle, blister, then turn a deep golden colour. Alternatively, use a deep-fryer and cook in batches of 6–8. Using a slotted spoon or tongs, transfer to a plate covered with crumpled kitchen paper and drain. Keep them hot in the oven while you cook the remainder.

Serve 5 parcels per person, with a choice of dipping sauces.

Traditionally filled with pork or bean paste, these fluffy buns are a popular and comforting dim sum. For a whiter bun, you can replace half the flour with potato flour, but the dough is less elastic, which makes it much harder to handle.

little szechuan chicken steamed buns

4 chicken thighs

3 tablespoons dark soy sauce

2 tablespoons clear honey

1 tablespoon Chinese rice wine (*Shaohsing*) or dry sherry

1–2 tablespoons hot chilli sauce

2–3 garlic cloves, crushed

1 tablespoon Szechuan peppercorns, crushed

Fluffy dough

230 g plain flour

3 teaspoons baking powder

2 tablespoons caster sugar

½ teaspoon salt

80 ml milk

3 tablespoons peanut oil

flour, for dusting

24 pieces non-stick baking parchment, 4 cm square

a bamboo steamer

Makes 24

Put the chicken into a large baking dish. Put the soy sauce into a bowl and mix in the honey, Chinese rice wine or sherry, chilli sauce, garlic and peppercorns. Pour over the chicken and turn to coat. Cover with foil or a lid and let marinate in the refrigerator for 30 minutes to 2 hours.

Transfer, still covered, to a preheated oven at 180°C (350°F) Gas 4 and roast for 20 minutes, then uncover and cook for a further 20 minutes. Let cool, remove the meat from the bones, shred finely and mix with any marinade and juices left in the baking dish.

To make the dough, put the flour into a large bowl and mix in the baking powder, sugar and salt. Stir in the milk, oil and 60 ml water to form a dough. Turn the dough onto a lightly floured board and knead for 5 minutes until it becomes elastic. Cover with a damp cloth and let rest at room temperature for 1 hour.

Divide the dough into 24 pieces and cover with a damp cloth. Take 1 piece of dough and, using your fingers, shape into a 6 cm disc. Put 1 teaspoon of the chicken filling in the centre and gather up the dough around it. Pinch the edges together and twist to seal. Put, sealed edges up, onto a square of non-stick baking parchment, cover, and repeat with the remaining dough and filling.

Put the buns into a bamboo steamer, 2 cm apart, and steam over gently simmering water for 15–20 minutes*. Transfer to a serving plate and serve.

*Note You can steam the buns the day before, then keep them well wrapped and chilled in the refrigerator. Re-steam them for 5 minutes before serving.

sushi

Homemade sushi tastes much more delicious than the shop-bought variety and is also very easy to make. First, cook the rice correctly, then you can follow our step-by-step method to make *norimaki* or rolled sushi. Other popular sushi include *nigiri*, an egg-shaped ball of rice topped with wasabi and raw fish, and *oshi*, rice and toppings pressed into a box, then unmoulded and cut into squares. Modern California rolls are sheets of nori with sushi rice, avocado and crab.

sushi rice

The major requirement is proper rice – aromatic Japanese sushi rice that will stick together. Sushi rice and the sushi rolling mats are sold in supermarkets, specialist food shops and Asian markets, which also sell special sushi fillings. Rice should always be measured by volume, not weight, and sushi rice should never be refrigerated, or it will become hard and unappetizing. That's why homemade sushi or sushi from Japanese restaurants is so much better than the commercial kind.

500 ml sushi rice

Sushi vinegar

140 ml Japanese rice vinegar

5 tablespoons sugar

4 teaspoons sea salt

6 cm fresh ginger, peeled, grated, then squeezed in a garlic crusher

3 garlic cloves, crushed

Makes 2 sushi rolls, 6 slices each

Wash the rice 5 times in cold water. Let drain in a strainer for at least 30 minutes, or overnight.

Transfer the rice to a saucepan and add 580 ml water (the same volume as the rice, plus 15 per cent extra). Cover tightly and bring to the boil over high heat. Reduce the heat to medium and simmer for 10 minutes. Reduce the heat to low and simmer for 5 minutes. Do not raise the lid. Still covered, let rest for 10 minutes.

Put the rice vinegar, sugar, salt, ginger and garlic into a separate saucepan and stir over low heat.

Put the rice into a wide, shallow dish and spread out. Cut through with a rice paddle or wooden spoon and fan to cool. Add the vinegar mixture and cut it through the rice with the spoon.

Use immediately while still tepid. Do not chill – cold spoils the taste and texture of sushi and the rice contains vinegar, which will preserve it for a short time.

The rice is now ready to be assembled into sushi, with various fillings and toppings. For a party, prepare at least 3 kinds, with one of each per person.

*Note Sushi rice can be very sticky. To make it easier to handle, the Japanese dip their hands in 'hand vinegar' first. Just pour some water into a bowl and add a splash of vinegar. Dip your fingers in the water before handling the rice.

Variation

Wipe 1 sheet of kombu seaweed with a cloth, slash it several times with a knife, then add it to the rice cooking water. Bring slowly to the boil, then discard the seaweed just before the water reaches boiling point.

making simple rolls *step-by-step*
cucumber sushi

1 sheet nori seaweed, briefly toasted over a gas flame or under a broiler

1 quantity sushi rice (page 31)

½ teaspoon wasabi paste

1 mini cucumber, deseeded and sliced lengthways into strips

To serve

Japanese soy sauce (*shoyu*)

pickled ginger

wasabi paste

a bamboo sushi rolling mat

Makes 12

Using a sharp knife, cut the seaweed in half. Put 1 piece onto a bamboo sushi mat, shiny side down. Divide the rice in half and press each half into a cylinder shape. Put one of the cylinders into the centre of the seaweed and press the rice outward until it meets the front edge. Press towards the far edge, leaving about 1–2 cm bare.

Brush ¼ teaspoon of wasabi paste down the centre of the rice and put a line of cucumber on top.

Roll up the mat gently starting from the front edge, pinching the roll together as you go. Complete the roll and squeeze firmly. Make a second cylinder using the remaining ingredients.

The sushi can be wrapped in plastic and left like this until you are ready to cut.

sushi allsorts: fillings and toppings

Instead of cucumber, use your choice of one or several of the ingredients listed below and arrange them in a line across the rice, 3 cm from the front edge. If using more than two fillings, use a whole sheet of seaweed instead of half. The roll is completed and cut as in the main recipe:

• Spring onions, finely sliced lengthways
• Carrots, finely sliced into matchsticks, then blanched
• Daikon (white radish or mooli), finely sliced lengthways into matchsticks
• Cucumber, deseeded and sliced lengthways
• Green beans or snake beans (Chinese yard-long beans), blanched
• Red and/or yellow peppers, deseeded and sliced into strips
• Trout or salmon caviar
• Smoked fish, cut into long shreds
• Very fresh fish fillets, sliced into strips and marinated in lime juice or rice vinegar for 30 minutes
• Cooked prawns, shelled, deveined and halved lengthways
• Raw or char-grilled tuna, finely sliced
• 3 eggs, beaten, cooked as a very thin omelette, then finely sliced
• Baby spinach leaves, blanched
• Avocado, finely sliced lengthways.

To serve, cut in half with a wet knife and trim off the end.

Cut each half in 3 and arrange on a serving platter. Small dishes of Japanese soy sauce (*shoyu*), pickled ginger and wasabi paste are traditional accompaniments.

palm sugar

1 cylinder palm sugar or
2 tablespoons brown sugar

If using palm sugar (available from specialist Asian food shops), put it onto a board and shave off shards with a sharp knife – enough to half-fill a small bowl.

red chilli flakes

a large handful of large dried red chillies

Put the chillies into a dry frying pan and heat gently until aromatic. Take care, because they burn easily.

Put the chillies into a small food processor and crush into flakes. Alternatively, use a mortar and pestle. To be authentic, keep the seeds in the mixture, but, if you prefer, remove as many as possible before crushing. Serve the flakes in a small bowl.

chilli fish sauce

3 fresh red bird's eye chillies, finely sliced crossways

125 ml Vietnamese or Thai fish sauce

Put the sliced chillies and fish sauce into a mixing bowl, stir briefly with a spoon, then transfer to a small bowl.

chilli vinegar sauce

125 ml white rice vinegar

3 fresh green bird's eye chillies, finely sliced crossways

Put the vinegar and chillies into a small screw-top jar, shake to mix, then set aside. When ready to serve, transfer to a small bowl.

thai condiments

South-east Asian homes and restaurants don't usually keep salt and freshly ground black pepper on the table. Instead, they have a 'cruet' of condiments, such as this one from Thailand. They include toasted dried red chilli flakes, sugar – usually palm sugar – and chillies steeped in fish sauce and vinegar, plus a separate bowl of chopped peanuts. Serve these condiments as great accompaniments to many Thai dishes, including noodles.

sweet chilli sauce

Sweet chilli sauce is a favourite Thai accompaniment for chicken, but is also very good with seafood, vegetables and meat. Use large chillies, rather than the tiny hot bird's eye chillies – they are milder so you can use more of them and achieve a more vibrantly coloured sauce.

250 g sugar

1 cup white rice vinegar

3–5 garlic cloves, crushed

4 fresh red chillies, deseeded and finely chopped

3 cm fresh ginger, peeled and grated

500 ml preserving bottle or jar, sterilized (page 4)

Makes 500 ml

Put the sugar and vinegar into a saucepan and bring to the boil, stirring until the sugar has dissolved.

Simmer for 10 minutes, then add the garlic, chillies and ginger. Cook for a further 5 minutes, then transfer to a sterilized bottle or jar and seal.

soy and ginger sauce

Soy and ginger make a great accompaniment to plain foods such as rice and vegetables that need extra seasoning. This sauce is best used within a few hours of making.

60 ml light soy sauce

60 ml dark soy sauce

5 cm fresh ginger, peeled and grated

1–2 tablespoons Chinese rice wine (*Shaohsing*) or dry sherry (optional)

Makes about 125 ml

Mix all the ingredients in a small bowl, then serve or set aside until required.

plum sauce

Though spicy, this sauce isn't hot. It goes wonderfully with meaty dim sum and keeps for months in sterilized jars.

1 kg plums, quartered and pitted

250 g brown sugar

1 tablespoon Szechuan peppercorns, pan-toasted

1 tablespoon fennel seeds, pan-toasted

1 teaspoon whole cloves

2–3 whole star anise

1 cinnamon stick, crushed

5 cm fresh ginger, peeled and grated

375 ml white rice vinegar

3 preserving bottles or jars, 250 ml each, sterilized (page 4)

Makes 750 ml

Put all the ingredients into a large saucepan and bring to the boil, stirring. Reduce to a steady simmer and cook for about 20 minutes until the plums have broken down.

Using the back of a wooden spoon, press the mixture through a sieve to remove the spices and plum skins, then pour into sterilized bottles or jars and seal.

sweet and sour sesame sauce

This sauce will keep for up to a month in a sterilized jar – sprinkle with sesame seeds just before serving.

100 g sugar

125 ml white rice vinegar

juice and grated zest of 1 lime

1–2 teaspoons dried chilli flakes

1 tablespoon sesame seeds, pan-toasted

125 ml preserving bottle or jar, sterilized (page 4)

Makes 125 ml

Put the sugar, vinegar, lime juice and zest, and chilli flakes into a medium saucepan and bring to the boil, stirring. Simmer for 5 minutes, or until reduced by half. Let cool, then pour into a serving bowl and sprinkle with the sesame seeds. Alternatively, pour into a sterilized bottle or jar and seal.

soups &salads

Soups are ubiquitous all over Asia – eaten for breakfast in Vietnam, or at the end of a meal instead of pudding in Japan. Salads are enthusiastically spicy, sweet and sour in Thailand, or elegantly simple in Japan.

Alter the vegetable components of this salad according to what's in season. Try broccoli or carrots sliced lengthways into matchsticks, spinach leaves, sliced Chinese cabbage or cauliflower florets. Snake beans (Chinese yard-long beans) rather than ordinary beans are ideal for salads, because they keep their crunch better.

indonesian gado-gado

2 mini cucumbers, such as Lebanese, halved lengthways and deseeded

8 snake beans (Chinese yard-long beans) or green beans, cut into 5 cm lengths

1 orange or red pepper

2 blocks firm beancurd (tofu), drained and dusted with cornflour

20–25 prawn crackers

2 onions, finely sliced into rings

a large handful of beansprouts, rinsed and trimmed

2 heads Little Gem lettuce, leaves separated

15 cm daikon (white radish or mooli), peeled and grated

2 hard-boiled eggs, quartered

sea salt flakes

peanut oil, for frying

Peanut sauce

250 g shelled fresh peanuts

2 fresh red chillies, halved, deseeded and finely chopped

2 fresh bird's eye chillies, halved, deseeded and finely chopped

1 onion, finely chopped

1 garlic clove, crushed

1 teaspoon sea salt

2 teaspoons brown sugar

200 ml coconut milk

Serves 4

To make the sauce, put the peanuts into a dry frying pan and toast. Transfer to a tea towel, rub off the skins, then put the nuts into a blender and grind to a coarse meal. Add the chillies, onion, garlic, salt, sugar and coconut milk, and process until smooth. Transfer to a saucepan and cook, stirring, until thickened.

Using a sharp knife, finely slice the halved cucumbers diagonally. Put onto a large plate, sprinkle with salt, let stand for 10 minutes, then rinse and pat dry with kitchen paper. Chill in the refrigerator until ready to serve.

Bring a saucepan of lightly salted water to the boil. Add the beans and cook until *al dente*. Drain, rinse immediately under cold running water and transfer to a bowl of iced water. Just before serving, drain again and pat dry with kitchen paper. Peel the pepper with a vegetable peeler, cut off and discard the top and base, then halve, deseed and finely slice lengthways.

Heat 2 tablespoons of peanut oil in a frying pan, add the beancurd and cook until browned on both sides, then drain and slice thickly.

To cook the crackers, fill a wok one-third full with peanut oil and heat to 190°C (375°F), or until a cracker puffs up immediately. Add the crackers and cook until puffed and golden, about 3 seconds. Remove with a slotted spoon and drain on kitchen paper.

To cook the onion rings, reheat the oil in the wok, add the onion rings and fry until crisp and golden. Remove with a slotted spoon and drain on kitchen paper.

Arrange the cucumbers, snake beans, pepper, beancurd, beansprouts, lettuce, daikon and quartered eggs on a large serving plate. Top with the onion rings and crackers, drizzle with the peanut sauce, sprinkle with salt and serve.

thai spicy prawn salad

1 tablespoon peanut oil

12 uncooked prawns, shelled, deveined and halved lengthways

1 stalk of lemongrass, very finely chopped

a handful of fresh coriander leaves, finely chopped

2 pink Thai shallots or 1 small regular shallot, finely sliced lengthways

3 spring onions, finely chopped

1 fresh red chilli, finely sliced and deseeded, if preferred

2 fresh kaffir lime leaves, mid-rib removed, the leaves very finely sliced crossways, then finely chopped

12 cherry tomatoes, halved

a handful of fresh mint sprigs, to serve

Thai dressing

4 tablespoons Vietnamese or Thai fish sauce

juice of 1 lemon or 2 limes

2 teaspoons brown sugar

2 tablespoons Thai red curry paste

Serves 4

A simple salad that could also be made with cooked prawns. When preparing the lemongrass and kaffir lime leaves, be sure to slice them very finely indeed. If you can't find them, use a squeeze of lemon juice and some grated lime zest instead.

Heat the peanut oil in a large wok, add the prawns and stir-fry for about 1 minute until opaque. Remove to a plate and let cool.

Put all the dressing ingredients into a large bowl and, using a fork, beat well until the sugar dissolves. Add the prawns and the remaining ingredients, except the mint. Toss well, then transfer to a large serving bowl, top with mint and serve.

Thai salads are incredibly easy to make, and absolutely packed with flavour. Don't worry if you can't find all these ingredients – ring the changes according to whatever is available. Use shredded barbecued pork, chicken or duck breast instead of the prawns, if you prefer. Rice vermicelli is like fine spaghetti – rice sticks are like strappy fettuccine. Obviously, increase quantities for more servings.

thai noodle salad
with shiitakes and chilli dressing

1 tablespoon sesame seeds

1 bundle rice stick or vermicelli noodles

sprigs of fresh coriander

Your choice of

½ green mango or green papaya

½ baby cucumber

2 fresh shiitake mushrooms

1 clump enokitake mushrooms

1 handful of beansprouts, trimmed

½ Asian pear (*nashi*) or regular pear, sliced lengthways

3 cherry tomatoes, halved

3 cooked tiger prawns, shelled

2.5 cm daikon (white radish or mooli), peeled and finely sliced

Chilli dressing

1 teaspoon chilli oil

1 teaspoon Vietnamese or Thai fish sauce

2 teaspoons lime juice

1 teaspoon vegetable oil

½ teaspoon soy sauce

½ teaspoon sugar

Serves 1

Put the sesame seeds into a dry frying pan and stir-fry for 1–2 minutes until golden. Set aside. Put all the dressing ingredients into a small bowl or screw-top jar and mix together.

Put the rice stick or vermicelli noodles into a bowl and pour over enough boiling water to cover. Let soak for 10 minutes for rice sticks, or 3 minutes for vermicelli. Drain thoroughly, rinse in cold water, then drain again. Return to the bowl and cover with iced water and ice cubes. Drain just before serving.

If using mango or papaya, peel with a vegetable peeler, then slice the flesh diagonally into strips. If using baby cucumber cut in half lengthways and, using a teaspoon, scoop out the seeds.

Using a vegetable peeler, peel the cucumber, leaving strips of green, then slice finely diagonally. If using shiitake mushrooms, remove and discard the stems and slice the caps crossways into 4–6 pieces. If using enokitake mushrooms, cut off and discard the roots and pull the clump apart.

Tip the dressing into a large serving bowl, add the drained noodles, toss, then top with your choice of ingredients. Sprinkle with the reserved toasted sesame seeds and coriander sprigs, and serve.

vietnamese salad wraps
with herbs, vegetables and noodles

A do-it-yourself salad platter is served with every Vietnamese meal. Some people think the idea was borrowed from the French, but in fact it is indigenous. The combinations of vegetables are almost infinite and the herbs give a fresh, scented flavour. To eat, take a lettuce leaf from the platter, add your choice of herbs and other ingredients, wrap the leaf into a parcel and dip in the spicy sauce.

2 teaspoons white rice vinegar

2 teaspoons sugar

½ teaspoon sea salt

2 large carrots, cut into matchsticks

about 20 cm cucumber, halved lengthways

60 g beanthread (cellophane) noodles (optional)*

4 Little Gem lettuces or 1 iceberg lettuce, leaves separated

6 spring onions, shredded

a handful of beansprouts, rinsed and trimmed

a large bunch of fresh coriander

a large bunch of fresh mint, leaves only

1 bunch of fresh Thai basil – not sweet basil, leaves only (optional)

Dipping sauce

2 garlic cloves, crushed

2 fresh red chillies, deseeded and sliced

1 tablespoon brown sugar

juice of ½ lime

4 tablespoons Vietnamese or Thai fish sauce

Serves 4

Put the vinegar, sugar and salt into a bowl, add 250 ml water and the strips of carrot, stir well and set aside for 30 minutes or up to 24 hours. Drain.

Using a sharp knife, finely slice the cucumber halves diagonally into half-moons.

If using noodles, bring a large saucepan of water to the boil, add the noodles and stir to separate. Boil for 2 minutes, then drain. Transfer the noodles to a bowl and cover with iced water and ice cubes until ready to use.

To make the dipping sauce, mash the garlic, 1 chilli and sugar to a paste with a mortar and pestle. Stir in the lime juice, fish sauce and 4 tablespoons of water. Taste and add extra water, if preferred, then pour into a small dipping bowl. Add the remaining chilli and set aside until ready to serve.

Arrange the lettuce leaves in the centre of a large serving platter, then put piles of carrots, cucumber, spring onions, beansprouts and herbs around the outside. Drain the noodles, and put into a separate bowl.

To eat, take a lettuce leaf, add your choice of other ingredients, then roll up. Dip in the dipping sauce and eat.

***Note** Noodles are sold loose in packets, in quantities suitable for a large number of people. You can also buy packets of noodles wrapped into balls, about 30 g each, 6–8 to a pack. These are perfect 1-person size – good for use in a noodle soup or similar dish, and are much easier to handle.

vietnamese chicken salad

4 handfuls of beansprouts,
rinsed and trimmed

1 baby carrot

6 spring onions, halved, then finely
sliced lengthways

1 handful of fresh mint leaves,
preferably Vietnamese mint

1 handful of fresh Thai basil leaves (optional)

2 tablespoons roasted peanuts,
finely chopped

Poached chicken

2 chicken breasts, on the bone

3 cm fresh ginger, peeled and sliced

1 garlic clove, crushed

1 tablespoon Vietnamese or Thai fish sauce,
or a pinch of salt

1 fresh red chilli, sliced

2 spring onions, sliced

boiling chicken stock or water, to cover

Chilli-lime dressing

75 ml freshly squeezed lime juice,
about 2–3 limes

1 tablespoon Vietnamese or Thai fish sauce

2 tablespoons brown sugar

1 fresh green chilli, halved, deseeded
and finely chopped

1 fresh red chilli, halved, deseeded
and finely chopped

1 garlic clove, crushed

3 cm fresh ginger, peeled and grated

Serves 4

You can use any cooked chicken for this salad. However, poaching is a very healthy way of cooking: there is no added fat, and much of what is there melts away as the chicken cooks. To be authentic, this salad should be made using stir-fried chicken mince, but this version is easy and tastes fresh and good, like most Vietnamese food. If you can't find Vietnamese mint and Thai basil, you can substitute ordinary mint, but not ordinary basil (just leave it out).

To poach the chicken, put the breasts into a wide saucepan, add the ginger, garlic, fish sauce or salt, chilli and spring onions. Cover with boiling chicken stock or water and return to the boil. Reduce the heat to low, cover with a lid and simmer, without boiling, until the chicken is tender, about 15–20 minutes. Remove from the heat and let cool in the liquid. Remove from the liquid, take the meat off the bone, discard the bone and skin, then pull the chicken into long shreds. Set aside the cooking liquid for another use, such as soup.

Put all the dressing ingredients into a screw-top jar and shake well.

To trim the beansprouts, pinch off the tails and remove the bean from between the 2 leaves (optional)*.

To prepare the carrot, peel and cut into long matchsticks on a mandoline, the large blade of a box grater, or a vegetable peeler.

Pile the beansprouts onto 4 serving plates. Add the carrot and chicken and top with the spring onions, mint and basil leaves, if using. Sprinkle with the dressing and roasted peanuts, then serve.

*__Note__ Trimming the bean out of the beansprout is optional, but generations of Chinese and Vietnamese grannies have insisted on it. They're right – it looks better and tastes better.

Soba noodles, made from buckwheat, are wonderful cold. Other Japanese noodles, such as white somen noodles or the larger, ribbon-like udon, are also delicious served this way. If you can find them, try the green tea-flavoured, pale green, cha-soba noodles (*cha* means 'tea' in many languages).

japanese soba noodle salad

400 g dried soba noodles

12 dried shiitake mushrooms

2 tablespoons Japanese soy sauce (*shoyu*)

2 tablespoons mirin (Japanese rice wine) or dry sherry

12 uncooked prawns

12 spring onions, finely sliced

4 teaspoons Japanese pepper mixture, such as furikake seasoning (optional)

4 teaspoons wasabi paste, to serve

Dipping sauce

250 ml dashi*

2 tablespoons mirin (Japanese rice wine) or dry sherry

a pinch of sugar

3 tablespoons Japanese soy sauce

Serves 4

*Dashi is available in powder or concentrate form in Chinese and Japanese shops. Dissolve 1 teaspoon in 1 cup of hot (not boiling) water, or to taste. To make your own dashi, see recipe page 140.

Put all the dipping sauce ingredients into a saucepan and simmer for 5 minutes. Chill in the refrigerator until required.

Bring a large saucepan of water to the boil, add the noodles and boil for about 5–6 minutes or according to the packet instructions. Drain, rinse in cold water, then drain again. Transfer the noodles to a bowl and cover with cold water and ice cubes. Chill in the refrigerator until required.

Put the shiitake mushrooms into a saucepan, cover with 250 ml boiling water and soak until soft. Remove and discard the mushroom stems. Add the soy sauce and mirin to the pan, bring to the boil and simmer for a few minutes to meld the flavours. Add the prawns and simmer for about 1 minute until opaque. Drain, reserving the cooking liquid. Shell the prawns, but leave the tail fins intact. Devein and split each prawn down the back to the fin, giving a butterfly shape. Chill the prawns and cooking liquid in the refrigerator. Just before serving, remove the prawns and dip the chilled noodles into the cooking liquid, then drain.

To serve, put a layer of ice cubes into bowl or a traditional slatted bamboo box, then add the noodles. Add the prawns, mushrooms and spring onions. Sprinkle with the pepper mixture, if using. Serve with wasabi and dipping sauce.

chinese crab and sweetcorn soup

Westerners serve soups at the beginning of a meal – in China, the opposite is the case. This recipe is one of the most familiar of all Chinese soups – delicious and easy to make. Fresh crabmeat and fresh sweetcorn cut straight from the cob will give the best flavour, but even if you have to use frozen ingredients, the soup will still be wonderful.

1 litre chicken stock

2 fresh ears of corn, or 250 g corn kernels, fresh or frozen and thawed

2 tablespoons cornflour

4 tablespoons Chinese rice wine (*Shaohsing*) or dry sherry

1 tablespoon light soy sauce

250 g crabmeat, fresh or frozen and thawed

2 teaspoons sesame oil

2 spring onions, finely sliced

a small bunch of fresh coriander, leaves only

25 g Chinese or regular cooked ham, chopped (optional)

sea salt and freshly ground white pepper

Serves 4–6

Pour the chicken stock into a large saucepan and bring to the boil.

If using fresh ears of corn, slice off the kernels with a sharp knife and discard the cob. Put the kernels into the stock. Return to the boil, then reduce the heat and simmer for 8–10 minutes.

Put the cornflour into a small bowl, then mix in the Chinese rice wine, soy sauce, salt and freshly ground white pepper. Stir into the saucepan of stock and return to the boil. Simmer for 5 minutes, then stir in the crabmeat, sesame oil, spring onions and coriander leaves. Cover the pan until the herbs turn vivid green, add the chopped ham, if using, heat through, then serve.

chinese treasure soup

You can buy Chinese barbecued duck and pork, but you can also make your own by rubbing with chilli oil or honey and Chinese five-spice powder, then roasting or grilling. Other treasures can be added to taste, including wontons filled with minced pork, fish or pork balls, and other vegetables, such as bok choy, pea shoots and bamboo shoots. The usual number of treasures is the magical eight.

½ Chinese barbecued duck, shredded

1 piece of Chinese barbecued pork spareribs, about 15 cm square, chopped into bite-sized pieces (optional)

1 carrot, finely sliced

6 uncooked prawns, shelled but with tail fins intact

2 sticks fried beancurd (tofu), sliced

2 Chinese cabbage leaves, sliced

1 handful of fresh bean sprouts, rinsed and trimmed

Wontons

250 g minced pork

3 canned bamboo shoots, chopped

a pinch of salt

1 packet wonton wrappers, about 12* (page 20)

1 egg white, beaten

Chinese stock

2 litres chicken stock

4 star anise

10 cm fresh ginger, peeled and finely sliced

1 onion, sliced

Serves 4

Warm the duck and pork in a preheated oven at 200°C (400°F) Gas 6 until completely heated through. (If cooking your own duck or pork, see the note below*.)

To make the wontons, mix the minced pork, bamboo shoots and salt in a bowl.

Take the wonton wrappers out of the plastic bag, but keep any you are not using covered with plastic as you work, because they dry out quickly.

Put 1 tablespoon of the pork mixture into the centre of each wonton wrapper and brush a circle of egg white around it. Twirl the wonton wrapper around the filling to make a shuttlecock shape.

Put all the stock ingredients into a saucepan and simmer for 30 minutes to meld the flavours. Pour the stock through a sieve to strain out the solids and return the stock to the rinsed-out pan. Return the stock to the boil and add the wontons, carrot and prawns. Simmer for about 3–5 minutes, or until the wontons rise to the surface and the filling is cooked.

Put the beancurd, cabbage, wontons and prawns into 4 large serving bowls, then pour over the boiling stock. Add the beansprouts, shredded duck and pork, then serve with chopsticks and Chinese spoons.

*Note If using char-grilled duck, rub 1 duck breast with Chinese five-spice powder and honey. Preheat a stove-top grill pan and cook, skin side down, until the fat begins to run. Pour off the fat at intervals, and continue cooking for about 20 minutes until the skin is crispy. Turn it over and cook the other side until brown – the centre will remain pink. Set aside to set the juices, then cut crossways into 1 cm slices.

If cooking your own pork, brush with chilli oil and roast in a preheated oven at 240°C (475°F) Gas 9 until very crisp. Set aside to set the juices, then slice into bite-sized pieces.

vietnamese watercress soup

2 tablespoons peanut oil

12 uncooked prawns, shelled but with shells reserved*

2.5 cm fresh ginger, peeled and grated

3 garlic cloves, finely sliced

1 stalk of lemongrass, trimmed, halved lengthways and lightly crushed

1 litre boiling fish stock

8 spring onions, white and green, halved crossways and bruised

2 tablespoons Vietnamese or Thai fish sauce

1 tablespoon sugar

1 teaspoon salt

a large bunch of watercress, trimmed

Serves 4

In Vietnam, this simple traditional soup is made with chrysanthemum leaves, and if you have access to a good specialist Asian food shop, you can try it made in the classic way. Watercress, with its peppery flavour and the texture contrast between the soft leaves and crunchy stems, is a good substitute. Add it at the very end, because it wilts very fast. If fish sauce is hard to find, use extra salt instead.

Heat the peanut oil in a wok, add the prawn shells, ginger, garlic and lemongrass and stir-fry until the shells change colour. Keep stir-frying for a few minutes to extract some of the flavour and colour. Transfer to the pan of boiling fish stock.

Add the spring onions to the wok and stir-fry for 2 minutes. Add the shelled prawns and stir-fry until they become opaque. Add the fish sauce, sugar and salt, then strain in the fish stock and return to the boil.

Divide the spring onions and prawns between 4 large soup bowls, then ladle in the stock. Add large handfuls of watercress and serve immediately.

*Note The prawn shells are included in this recipe because they give terrific flavour. If your prawns are already shelled, omit this step and stir-fry the ginger, garlic and lemongrass at the same time as the prawns, then remove the lemongrass and ginger before serving. You can also use cooked, shelled prawns, instead of raw ones, adding them at the same time as the stock. For a more substantial soup, add your choice of soaked or fresh noodles with the stock.

singapore laksa

2 tablespoons corn or peanut oil

500 ml coconut milk

500 ml boiling fish or chicken stock

1 cooked chicken breast, shredded

2 fried Chinese fishcakes, sliced (optional)

12 uncooked prawns (optional)

200 g somen or cellophane (beanthread) noodles, soaked according to the packet instructions

6 spring onions

1 bunch of fresh coriander

4 handfuls of beansprouts, rinsed and trimmed

a bunch of fresh mint or Vietnamese mint

Spice paste

3 stalks of lemongrass, sliced

4 garlic cloves, sliced

3 cm fresh ginger, peeled and sliced

3 shallots or 6 Thai shallots, chopped

8 blanched almonds or 4 candlenuts

3 fresh red chillies, deseeded

1 teaspoon ground turmeric

1 teaspoon salt

1 teaspoon sugar, preferably brown

Serves 4

Laksas are found in different forms all over the Malay peninsula. In Penang they are almost overpoweringly fishy, while in Singapore they can be very spicy – this version is milder. You can vary the ingredients according to what's available in the market, and to suit your own taste – but the basics should be a truly wonderful, flavourful stock, plus noodles. The spice paste can also be simplified by using a ready-made Thai paste instead, though the true laksa pastes are sometimes available in the South-east Asian sections of Chinese supermarkets.

Put all the spice paste ingredients into a spice grinder or blender and grind until smooth, adding a little oil, if necessary. Heat the oil in a wok, add the paste and stir-fry for 6–8 minutes without burning. Add the coconut milk and stock and simmer gently for 5 minutes to develop the flavours.

Add the chicken, fishcakes and prawns, if using, and simmer for 2 minutes or until the prawns become opaque. Prepare the noodles according to the packet instructions. Using a slotted spoon, divide the noodles, chicken, fishcakes and prawns between 4 large serving bowls, then add the spring onions, coriander, beansprouts and mint. Pour over the coconut stock and serve immediately.

malay chicken soup

2 bundles beanthread (cellophane) or rice noodles such as *ho fun* or *bahn pho*, fresh or dried

1.5 litres Asian chicken stock (page 66) or water

1.5 kg whole chicken or 750 g boneless, skinless chicken breasts

about 250 g green beans or snake beans (Chinese yard-long beans), cut into 7 cm lengths

1 carrot, finely sliced

1 courgette, finely sliced

2 tablespoons peanut oil

sea salt and freshly ground black pepper

Spice paste

2 stalks of lemongrass

2 tablespoons black pepper, coarsely cracked

2 tablespoons Vietnamese or Thai fish sauce, or 1 teaspoon shrimp paste (*blachan* or *belacan*), toasted

2 teaspoons ground turmeric

8 pink Thai shallots or 2 onions, finely chopped

3 cm fresh ginger, peeled and grated

6 garlic cloves, crushed

a large handful of blanched almonds

To serve

4 spring onions, finely sliced

4 fresh red chillies, deseeded and finely sliced

a handful of baby mushrooms (optional)

2 lemons, cut into wedges

Serves 4

You find soups like this in Malaysia, Indonesia and other parts of South-east Asia. Use a whole chicken to make the stock, then remove the skin and bone and shred the meat. Alternatively, use ready-made stock, and poach the chicken breasts separately. Use beanthread (cellophane) or rice vermicelli noodles, not wheat-based ones. Any number of vegetables may be added. You can use a ready-made Thai spice paste for convenience, but a blender makes this one in a minute.

If using dried noodles, put them into a bowl and pour over enough hot water to cover. Let soak for 30 minutes, then drain and keep in cold water until required. If using fresh noodles, separate them into strips, then put into a bowl and pour over enough hot water to cover. Let soak for a few minutes, drain and keep in cold water until required.

Put the chicken stock or water into a large stockpot and bring to the boil. Add the chicken (add more boiling water if the bird is not completely covered by liquid). Poach gently until the chicken is tender, about 1 hour. Transfer the chicken to a plate, let cool, discard the skin and bones, then, using a sharp knife, shred the flesh into long strips. If using chicken breasts, bring the stock to the boil, add the chicken breasts and poach until tender, about 15 minutes. Remove the chicken from the stock and shred. Return the stock to the boil, add the beans and carrot and simmer until *al dente*. Remove with a slotted spoon and plunge them into a bowl of iced water. Add the courgette to the stock and blanch until tender, about 1 minute. Remove with a slotted spoon and add to the bowl of iced water. Set aside the stock. When all the vegetables are cold, remove them from the iced water, cover and set aside.

To make the spice paste, cut the top off the lemongrass with a sharp knife and keep just the white part. Peel off the 2 outer leaves, and finely slice the rest. Put into a small blender or food processor with the other spice paste ingredients and grind until a coarse paste forms. Alternatively, use a mortar and pestle. Set aside.

Heat the peanut oil in a wok, add the spice paste and fry until fragrant. Add the stock, chicken, beans, carrot and courgette and heat until very hot. Taste and adjust the seasoning. Drain the noodles and divide between 4 serving bowls. Ladle the chicken, vegetables and stock over the noodles and serve, topped with the spring onions, chillies and mushrooms, if using. Serve with lemon wedges for squeezing.

This must be one of the world's best-loved soups – utterly superb. Fresh lemongrass, galangal (like fresh ginger, but crisper and more medicinal), kaffir lime leaves and fiery bird's eye chillies will require a visit to a Thai or Chinese grocer or supermarket. Powdered substitutes will not do. Buy extra of these fresh ingredients and freeze for later.

spicy thai chicken soup

1.25 litres boiling chicken stock, preferably homemade

350 g boneless, skinless chicken breasts, finely sliced

2 garlic cloves, chopped

2 stalks of lemongrass, halved lengthways

3 tablespoons Vietnamese or Thai fish sauce, or light soy sauce

3 cm fresh ginger, peeled and grated

3 cm fresh galangal, peeled and sliced (optional)

8 small spring onions, quartered

250 ml canned coconut milk

4 fresh kaffir lime leaves, crushed (optional)

2 fresh green bird's eye chillies, crushed

a large handful of fresh coriander leaves, torn

250 g uncooked tiger prawns, tails only, shelled or unshelled*

freshly squeezed juice of 2 limes

Serves 4

Do not use cooked prawns as the texture will be disappointing.

Put the chicken stock into a large saucepan and bring to the boil. Add the chicken, garlic, lemongrass, fish sauce or soy sauce, ginger, galangal, if using, spring onions and coconut milk.

Return to the boil, part-cover, then reduce the heat to a high simmer and cook for 5 minutes. Add the kaffir lime leaves, if using, the chillies, half the coriander leaves and the prawns.

Simmer gently for 5 minutes, or until the chicken is cooked through and the prawn flesh is opaque – do not overcook or the prawns will be tough. Add the lime juice and serve in 4 large soup bowls, topped with the remaining coriander leaves.

*Note Remove the chillies before eating the soup: they are fiery, but leaving them whole and merely crushing them releases a gentle, not violent heat.

A variation on a traditional Japanese summer soup, prized for the fresh taste of sweetcorn – and very easy to make.

japanese fresh corn soup
with spring onions and tamari soy sauce

4 fresh whole ears of corn, husks and silks removed, or about 500 g fresh or frozen corn kernels

1 litre hot dashi* or chicken stock

To serve

4 egg yolks (optional)

4 spring onions, sliced diagonally

2 tablespoons tamari or dark soy sauce

cracked black pepper or a Japanese pepper mixture, such as furikake seasoning or seven-spice (*sichimi togarashi*)

Serves 4

*Dashi is sold in powder or concentrate form in many supermarkets and specialist Asian food shops. For a recipe to make your own, see page 140.

Bring a large saucepan of water to the boil, add the ears of corn and simmer for about 15 minutes. Drain. Hold the ears upright on a chopping board, blunt end down and run a sharp knife down the cobs, shaving off the kernels.

Put the kernels into a blender with 250 ml dashi* or chicken stock and process until smooth. Using the back of a wooden spoon, press through a sieve into a saucepan. Return the corn to the blender, add another ladle of stock, process until smooth, then strain as before, pushing through as much corn juice as possible. Repeat until all the stock has been used. Reheat the mixture.

Divide the egg yolks, if using, between 4 small soup bowls, ladle the soup on top and beat with chopsticks (the hot soup cooks the egg). Serve, topped with spring onions, tamari or soy sauce and cracked black pepper to taste.

vegetables & vegetarian

Except for monks, few East and South-east Asians are exclusively vegetarian. That doesn't stop them creating some of the freshest, most healthful vegetable dishes on earth, and serving them with great respect for flavour and freshness.

chinese mushrooms
with spring onions and sesame seeds

There are so many wild and cultivated mushrooms available now that it seems a pity not to take advantage of them in stir-fries, where their form, colour and flavour is shown off to best advantage. A wonderful mixture is cooked here with the famous 'Chinese trinity' of stir-fry tastes – aromatic garlic, ginger and spring onions.

2 tablespoons sesame seeds

1 kg assorted mushrooms, such as fresh shiitakes, enokitakes, yellow or pink oyster mushrooms (but not grey!), plus other wild and cultivated mushrooms

2 tablespoons peanut oil

2 garlic cloves, crushed

3 cm fresh ginger, peeled and grated or finely sliced

6 spring onions, finely sliced

1 teaspoon sugar

2 teaspoons soy sauce

Serves 4

To prepare the sesame seeds, heat a small frying pan over medium heat (don't add any oil). Add the sesame seeds and toast gently until golden. Take care, because they burn easily. Transfer to a plate and let cool.

To prepare the mushrooms, remove the stems from the shiitakes and cut the caps in half. Slice off the end of the roots from the enokitake mushrooms and break the clumps into sections. Trim off the cut end of the roots from all the other mushrooms and brush the caps clean with a soft cloth. Leave the oyster mushrooms whole and slice the rest in half lengthways.

Heat the oil in a wok, add the garlic, ginger and spring onions and stir-fry for 20 seconds. Add the firmer kinds of mushrooms and stir-fry for a few minutes.

Add the sugar and soy sauce and stir-fry quickly until the sugar has been dissolved. Add the oyster and enokitake mushrooms, turning gently in the sauce without breaking them up. Transfer to a serving plate, sprinkle with the sesame seeds and serve immediately with rice or meat dishes.

stir-fried water chestnuts and sprouts

3 tablespoons peanut or safflower oil

2 garlic cloves, crushed

250 g baby Brussels sprouts, trimmed and halved

250 g canned water chestnuts, drained and sliced

50 ml Chinese rice wine (*Shaohsing*) or dry sherry

a pinch of salt

Serves 4

This is a Chinese-inspired variation on the French dish of Brussels sprouts and sweet chestnuts. Cabbagey things like sprouts should not be cooked longer than a few minutes, or they will punish you with a dreadful stink! This is the perfect solution to the problem.

Heat the peanut oil in a large wok, add the garlic and stir-fry quickly until golden. Add the sprouts and water chestnuts and stir-fry for a few seconds. Add the Chinese rice wine, salt and 125 ml water, cover the wok, reduce the heat and steam for 1–2 minutes, or until the sprouts are lightly cooked but not soft.

Serve immediately with other dishes as part of a Chinese meal, or as accompaniment to meat or poultry cooked in the Western style.

vietnamese stir-fried bok choy

2 tablespoons peanut or safflower oil

1 garlic clove, crushed

3 cm fresh ginger, peeled and grated

3 stalks of lemongrass, trimmed and finely sliced

2 spring onions, chopped

2 fresh red chillies, finely sliced

1 tablespoon Vietnamese or Thai fish sauce

1 tablespoon sugar

1 kg baby bok choy, halved lengthways

2 tablespoons Chinese rice wine (*Shaohsing*), or dry sherry

Serves 4

Stir-frying is the perfect way to preserve the taste, colour and nutrients of good fresh vegetables – and Asian cooks are past masters at the art.

Heat the peanut oil in a large wok, add the garlic, ginger, lemongrass, spring onions, chillies, fish sauce and sugar, and stir-fry for 1–2 minutes.

Add the bok choy and 1 tablespoon of water and stir-fry for 1 minute until the leaves are lightly wilted. Sprinkle with the Chinese rice wine, stir once and serve.

pattypan snake beans
in spicy coconut milk

10 snake beans (Chinese yard-long beans), cut in 5 cm lengths

125 g yellow and green pattypan squash, halved

8 yellow or green mini courgettes, halved lengthways

500 ml coconut milk

1 tablespoon Vietnamese or Thai fish sauce

1 tablespoon sugar

1 teaspoon dried chilli flakes (optional)

250 g sugar snap peas

8 ripe red or yellow cherry tomatoes, halved and deseeded

To serve

8 sprigs of fresh coriander

1 fresh red chilli, sliced

2 spring onions, sliced

Serves 4

This simple dish of South-east Asian flavours is an excellent way to serve vegetables – spicy, barely cooked, but bathed in coconut milk. This recipe uses pretty little pattypan squash, sugar snap peas and snake beans (Chinese yard-long beans), which keep their crunch and bite better than ordinary beans, but use whichever crisp vegetables are in season and freshest at the market.

Fill a large wok one-third full of lightly salted water and heat until boiling. Add the snake beans and cook for 1 minute until blanched. Remove with a slotted spoon, drain and set aside. Repeat with the pattypans and courgettes.

Discard the water and add the coconut milk, fish sauce, sugar and chilli flakes, if using, and heat, stirring, to boiling point.

Add all the vegetables and simmer, stirring, for 5 minutes or until heated through. Transfer to a serving bowl, sprinkle with sprigs of coriander, the sliced chilli and spring onion, and serve with other Asian dishes.

Note Coconut milk must be stirred as it heats, or it will curdle: similarly, it should never be covered with a lid.

vietnamese pancakes
with beansprouts and spring onions

The Vietnamese usually fill these pancakes with prawns, shredded duck or stir-fried pork strips as well as all the vegetables, and you could too. However, this vegetarian version is simply great! The pancakes can be served as part of a meal or eaten as a snack at any time of the day.

4 onions, finely sliced (optional)

20 fresh shiitake mushrooms, stems removed and discarded, caps sliced

2 large handfuls of beansprouts, rinsed and trimmed

1 fresh red chilli, finely sliced (optional)

peanut oil, for frying

Coconut pancakes

75 g rice flour

35 g cornflour

1 teaspoon ground turmeric

1 teaspoon sugar

8 spring onions, white and green parts sliced diagonally crossways

50 ml coconut milk

2 eggs, beaten

1 tablespoon Vietnamese or Thai fish sauce

To serve

lettuce leaves

sprigs of fresh Asian mint or Thai basil

sprigs of fresh coriander (optional)

Vietnamese or Thai fish sauce, *nuóc cham* (page 17) or chilli dipping sauce (page 10)

Serves 4

To make the pancakes, put the two flours, turmeric, sugar and spring onions into a bowl and, using a wooden spoon, mix well. Put the coconut milk, eggs, and fish sauce into a bowl and stir well, then gradually stir into the flour mixture to form a smooth batter. Set aside.

Heat 1 tablespoon of the oil in a wok, add the onions, if using, and stir-fry until soft and golden. Remove with a slotted spoon and set aside.

Add 1 teaspoon of the oil to the wok, swirl around to coat the surface and heat well. Pour one-quarter of the batter into the wok and swirl it around to coat the surface thinly. Put one-quarter of the mushrooms, beansprouts, chilli and onions, if using, into the centre of the pancake. Cover with a lid, turn the heat to low and cook for 3 minutes, or until the filling is heated through.

Using a spatula, fold the pancake in half like a French omelette, transfer to a serving plate and keep hot. Repeat until you have 4 pancakes.

Serve immediately with a separate plate of lettuce leaves, mint or basil, and coriander, if using. Each person puts a piece of the pancake in a lettuce leaf, adds sprigs of mint, basil or coriander, rolls up the leaf and eats it either plain or dipped into *nuóc cham* or chilli dipping sauce.

Vegetarian diets were never hugely popular in China. The monasteries were the main proponents of the vegetarian lifestyle – and there aren't many monks left in the People's Republic. However, this dish is so good that any meat would utterly ruin its flavour – and yet it has the satisfying effect of a meat dish.

monks' vegetables

½ Chinese cabbage, leaves separated

4 carrots, finely sliced diagonally

240 g canned sliced bamboo shoots, drained

150 g fresh shiitake mushrooms, halved

240 g canned sliced water chestnuts, drained

4 baby bok choy, halved lengthways

2 blocks firm beancurd (tofu), cut into 3 cm cubes

3 tablespoons cornflour, for dusting

peanut oil, for frying

boiled rice or noodles, to serve

Sauce

2 tablespoons yellow bean sauce, diluted with 6 tablespoons water

2 tablespoons light soy sauce

2 tablespoons dark soy sauce

2 tablespoons hoisin sauce

2 tablespoons sugar

200 ml water or vegetable stock

125 ml Chinese sweet rice wine (*Shaohsing*), or medium dry sherry

a Chinese sandpot or ceramic casserole dish

Serves 4

Bring a large saucepan of water to the boil, add the Chinese cabbage leaves and blanch for 1 minute. Remove, plunge into a large bowl of iced water, then drain. Using a sharp knife, cut out and discard the white stalks. Put the leaves one on top of the other on a dry cloth (arrange them with stalk ends on alternate sides), then roll up the leaves like a sushi into a cylinder and press hard to squeeze out the water. Remove from the cloth and cut the rolls into 5 cm lengths*. Set aside.

Heat 1 tablespoon of the peanut oil in a wok or frying pan until it begins to smoke. Stir-fry all the vegetables, except the cabbage and bok choy, one at a time in the order shown, transferring each one to a plate before adding the next. Add more oil as required and reheat it each time before frying the next batch.

Dust the beancurd with the cornflour, in several batches (do this just before frying). Fill a large wok or saucepan one-third full of the peanut oil and heat to 190°C (375°F), or until a piece of noodle puffs up immediately – it must be very hot or the beancurd will stick. Add the beancurd and fry until well browned. Remove with a slotted spoon and drain on kitchen paper.

Put a layer of fried beancurd into a Chinese sandpot or ceramic casserole dish. Add the carrots, bamboo shoots, mushrooms, water chestnuts, bok choy and cabbage rolls. Put the sauce ingredients into a jug or bowl and mix well. Pour over the vegetables, then cover with a lid and let marinate in the refrigerator for about 30 minutes, or until you are ready to cook the final dish.

Put the sandpot or casserole into a cold oven, turn the heat to 200°C (400°F) Gas 6 for about 20 minutes, or until boiling, then reduce the heat to 140°C (275°F) Gas 1 and simmer for 3 minutes to let the sauce bubble through. Serve immediately with rice or noodles.

*Note This cabbage preparation is based on a Japanese original, but is a terrific way to include lots of leaves in the dish without taking up huge amounts of room.

sweet and sour
pickled vegetables

In Chinese restaurants, the dim sum trolley holds a myriad exciting tastes and smells, and each should be appreciated individually. Chinese pickles are a wonderful way of cleansing the palate between bites. They also make a great accompaniment to many meat and fish dishes. Serve with a jar of chopsticks so guests can help themselves, or serve small portions wedged into joined wooden chopsticks (the disposable kind).

1 small cucumber, about 400 g or 20 cm

2 carrots, about 200 g

6 radishes, about 100 g, trimmed

8 cm fresh ginger, peeled

¼ Chinese or Savoy cabbage, about 150 g

3 tablespoons salt

6 dried red chillies (optional)

125 g sugar

500 ml white rice vinegar

4 tablespoons Chinese rice wine
(*Shaohsing*) or dry sherry, (optional)

1 litre glass preserving jar, sterilized (page 4)

Makes 750 ml

Using a sharp knife, cut the cucumber in half lengthways and scoop out the seeds with a teaspoon. Slice the cucumber, carrots, radishes and ginger lengthways into fine strips*.

Using a sharp knife, slice the cabbage into 1 cm strips. Bring a saucepan of water to the boil, then add the cabbage and blanch for 30 seconds. Drain and rinse in cold water.

Put the cucumber, carrots and radishes into a shallow glass or china dish and sprinkle with salt. Let stand for 10 minutes, then pat dry with kitchen paper.

Put all the vegetables, ginger and dried chillies, if using, into a sterilized jar.

Put the sugar, vinegar and Chinese rice wine, if using, into a medium saucepan and bring to the boil, stirring constantly. Reduce the heat and simmer for about 10 minutes. Remove from the heat and let cool.

When cool, pour over the vegetables and seal the sterilized jar. The pickles will keep in the refrigerator for 2 weeks. The cabbage will discolour after 2 days, but will still taste good.

*Note Use a mandoline to slice the vegetables; it makes the job easier and gives a more even result. (Inexpensive plastic Japanese mandolines are sold in kitchen shops and Asian markets, and by mail order.)

fish &seafood

Seafood in Asian street markets is incredibly fresh. You can see the fish jumping out of the baskets and the prawns hopping off down the road in search of safety. Mussels and clams squirt salty water at you as you make your choice.

japanese tempura

250 g uncooked king prawns, shelled and deveined

250 g squid caps, opened out flat

8 fresh shiitake or 100 g enokitake mushrooms

8 sprigs of fresh parsley with stalks

8 perilla (*shiso*), rocket or baby spinach leaves

flour, for coating

peanut oil, for frying

Dipping sauces

250 ml dashi* (page 65) or chicken stock

60 ml light soy sauce

2 tablespoons mirin (Japanese rice wine) or dry sherry

1 tablespoon caster sugar

2 tablespoons grated or sliced fresh ginger

10 cm daikon (white radish or mooli), grated

1 fresh red chilli, finely chopped

Tempura batter

1 egg yolk

100 g plain flour, sifted

Serves 4

Tempura was probably invented between 1550 and 1650 AD in Nagasaki, not by the Japanese, but by homesick Portuguese traders. It is a delicious dish in which a selection of food is covered with a light, lacy, airy batter and fried quickly, then served with a dipping sauce. It's now found all around the world and is perfect takeaway food.

The batter should be barely mixed: make half at a time, then mix a second batch for a crisp, fresh effect. Prawns and squid, as used here, taste and look good – add greens to balance the flavours. If you can't find perilla (*shiso*) leaves, use rocket or baby spinach. Have all the fish and seafood prepared, the dip made, the chilli-daikon mixture ready and the oil hot, then make and use the batter at the very end. This egg yolk tempura is the one preferred in Osaka – pale yellow, not white. In Tokyo, the batter is often made with egg white and is much paler.

Using a sharp knife, score the prawns several times on the underside to stop them curling. Cut the squid into even 5 cm squares and score them, criss-cross, on both sides. Remove the stems from the shiitakes and cut the caps in half. Assemble all the ingredients to be fried and dust them with flour.

To make the dipping sauce, put the dashi or chicken stock, soy sauce, mirin, sugar and ginger into a small bowl and mix well. Put the daikon and chilli into a separate small bowl and mix.

Fill a large wok or saucepan one-third full of oil and heat to 190°C (375°F), or until a piece of noodle puffs up immediately.

To make the batter, put the egg yolk into a bowl, add 125 ml iced water and, using a whisk, whisk 2–3 times only. Add the flour, mix again, minimally, until barely mixed and lumpy-looking. Using chopsticks, dip each piece into the batter, then cook in the hot oil. Do not cook more than 5 pieces at once or the temperature will drop. Remove each batch, drain on crumpled kitchen paper and keep hot in the oven while you cook the remainder. Serve with the chilli mixture and a bowl of dipping sauce.

This is a very elegant and stylish dish, and easy to make – the bowls can be assembled beforehand, then cooked at the very last minute. The traditional Japanese practice of salting the fish increases the succulence of its flesh when cooked – a great secret for all fish cooks!

japanese steamed fish
on noodles with seaweed

1 salmon fillet, about 500–750 g

1 bundle soba buckwheat noodles, about 125 g

1 bundle somen noodles, about 125 g

1 sheet kombu seaweed, wiped with a cloth, then cut into 4 pieces (optional)*

4 tablespoons sake

salt

Dashi sauce

250 ml dashi* (page 65)

175 ml mirin (Japanese rice wine)

175 ml Japanese soy sauce

a handful of dried bonito flakes (optional)

4 ceramic bowls with lids or 4 bowls

a bamboo steamer

Serves 4

Sprinkle a thick layer of salt on a plate. Using a sharp knife, cut the salmon crossways into 4 strips and put the pieces, skin side down, onto the plate. Set aside for 20 minutes, then rinse off the salt and pat dry with kitchen paper.

Bring a large saucepan of water to the boil, add the noodles and cook, stirring a little with chopsticks, until the water returns to the boil. Add a splash of cold water and return to the boil. Repeat this 2 more times, until the noodles are *al dente* – a total of 3–4 minutes. Drain, rinse under cold running water and set aside.

When ready to assemble, dip the noodles into boiling water and drain. Put pieces of kombu seaweed, if using, into 4 lidded ceramic bowls (or, use bowls with a small saucer as a lid). Add a pile of noodles and top with a fish fillet, skin side up.

Sprinkle 1 tablespoon of sake over each one, put a circle of foil on top and the lid on top of that. Put the bowls into 1 or more tiers of a bamboo steamer, then steam for about 10 minutes or until the fish is cooked, but still pink in the centre.

Put all the dashi sauce ingredients into a saucepan, bring to the boil and, when ready to serve, strain over the fish. Serve with chopsticks and small spoons.

*Note The kombu seaweed is there for flavour – discard before eating.

The Chinese use leftover rice in a variety of ways – fried rice is a favourite, but one that excites huge controversy and discussion. The secret is to use recently cooked rice, which is cool, rather than hot or cold, and it shouldn't be too damp or too dry either. Cooked this way, it can be in a class all by itself. This version is colourful, delicious and easy, and you can vary the components according to what's fresh and in season. Serve soy and chilli sauces separately.

chinese fried rice

4 tablespoons peanut oil

1 egg, beaten

1 onion, finely sliced

2 spring onions, finely sliced

2 garlic cloves, finely sliced

2.5 cm fresh ginger, peeled and finely sliced (optional)

425–450 g recently cooked white rice, at room temperature

125 g cooked asparagus or green beans, sliced into 3 cm pieces

125 g corn kernels (optional)

2 ripe red tomatoes, skinned, deseeded and chopped

350 g cooked chicken, shelled prawns or crabmeat, or a mixture of all three

To serve

soy sauce

sweet chilli sauce

Serves 4

Heat 2 tablespoons of the oil in a wok, swirl to coat, add the beaten egg and stir constantly until cooked and golden. Using a slotted spoon, remove the egg, slice finely, then set aside.

Heat the remaining oil in the wok, add the onion, spring onions, garlic, ginger, if using, and the cooked rice. Stir-fry for 2 minutes.

Add the asparagus or green beans, corn, if using, and tomatoes. Add 125 ml water, then the chicken, prawns or crabmeat, and the cooked egg. Cover the wok with a lid, reheat for about 1–2 minutes, then serve hot with little dishes of soy sauce and sweet chilli sauce.

malaysian penang tamarind fish laksa

Make spice pastes in quantity and freeze them – this one, or a ready-made Thai curry paste are all good. Tamarind gives a lemony taste.

500 g fresh udon noodles, or 250 g dried

1 litre fish stock or water

2.5 cm fresh ginger or galangal, peeled and grated

500 g boneless, skinless fish fillets

1 tablespoon tamarind paste*

1 teaspoon brown sugar

sea salt and freshly ground black pepper

Spice paste

3 dried chillies, deseeded and soaked

2 stalks of lemongrass, chopped

2.5 cm fresh ginger or galangal, peeled and grated

1 teaspoon ground turmeric

1 tablespoon shrimp paste (*blachan* or *belacan*)

12 spring onions, finely sliced

1 tablespoon peanut oil

To serve

8–12 cooked, shelled medium prawns (optional)

a bunch of fresh Vietnamese mint or mint

1 small packet beansprouts, rinsed and trimmed

a bunch of fresh coriander leaves, torn

2 fresh red chillies, deseeded and finely sliced

Serves 4

If using dried noodles, bring a large saucepan of lightly salted water to the boil. Add the noodles and cook for 10–12 minutes. If fresh, boil for 2–2½ minutes. During boiling, add a splash of cold water once or twice during the cooking time, then return to the boil. Drain thoroughly and keep in a bowl of cold water until ready to assemble the dish.

Put all the spice paste ingredients, except the peanut oil, into a blender, spice grinder or small food processor and process until smooth, adding a few tablespoons of water as necessary to make a paste. Heat the peanut oil in a wok, add the paste and stir-fry for about 6 minutes – the rawness should be cooked out of the spices.

Add the fish stock or water and ginger and heat until boiling. Add the fish, turn off the heat and cover with a lid. Leave for about 5 minutes until the fish is cooked, then break the fish into large pieces in the stock. Reheat to boiling point, then stir in the tamarind paste, sugar, salt and freshly ground black pepper.

Drain the noodles, then dunk them and the prawns, if using, into a bowl of boiling water until heated through. Drain again, then put a pile of the hot noodles into 4 large Chinese soup bowls, ladle the fish and stock over the top and sprinkle with mint, beansprouts, prawns, coriander and chillies.

*Note Tamarind paste is sold in bottles in specialist Asian food shops, and this is the most convenient form. Substitute the juice of 1 lime if you can't find it.

These rice flour pancakes are sometimes called 'Korean pizzas' by Korean expatriates – they are snack foods often served outdoors, at markets, fairs and celebrations. In this version oysters are used, but clams or abalone could also be included. Dip the torn or cut portions of the pancakes into the flavourful sauce before eating. Dried Korean chilli is sold as either shreds or grains – but you could also use chilli powder or crushed chillies.

korean oyster pancakes
with chilli-sesame dipping sauce

500 g fresh oysters or about 300 g canned oysters in brine, or other seafood

125 g rice flour

125 g plain white flour

½ teaspoon salt

1 large egg

1 teaspoon dark sesame oil

8–12 spring onions

4 tablespoons peanut oil, for frying

Chilli-sesame dipping sauce

6 tablespoons Japanese soy sauce (*shoyu*)

4 tablespoons Japanese rice vinegar

2 shallots, finely sliced

1 tablespoon sesame seeds, pan-toasted

½ teaspoon sliced fresh red chilli, crushed dried chillies or chilli powder

Serves 4

If using fresh oysters, shuck them and set aside the liquid from the shells. If using oysters in brine, drain them and set aside the brine. Make up the liquid to 250 ml with water. (If using smoked oysters in oil, discard the oil.)

Sift the flours and salt into a large bowl. Using a balloon whisk, whisk in the brine or oyster water, together with the egg and sesame oil, to form a thin, creamy batter. Let stand while you prepare the other ingredients.

Cut the spring onions in half crossways and slice the green parts into diagonal shreds. Cut the white parts lengthways into quarters.

To prepare the dipping sauce, put all the ingredients into a blender and mix briefly, then pour into 4 small serving dishes.

Heat 1 tablespoon of the peanut oil in a heavy-based frying pan or wok, swirling it around to coat well. Toss in one-quarter of the oysters and a few pieces of spring onion. Add one-quarter of the batter and some more of the spring onion. Cook the pancake for 4–5 minutes, turn it and cook for a further 3–4 minutes, until the surface is mottled with brown. Tear into 4 pieces and keep hot, while you cook the remaining pancakes, then serve with the chilli-sesame dipping sauce.

Banana leaves are the traditional wraps for this famous dish from Malaysia, but you could also use foil or greaseproof paper. Use a firm fish – though Malaysia doesn't have salmon, it is used here because it's widely available and marries well with spicy flavours. Be warned – this one's hot! If you want something less fiery, use fewer chillies.

otak otak *fish parcels*

600 g firm fish without bones, such as salmon, mackerel or cod

3 teaspoons salt

4 eggs

3 fresh kaffir lime leaves, central stems removed and remainder finely sliced

250 ml coconut cream

Chilli paste

5 dried chillies, soaked in boiling water for 15 minutes

5 fresh red bird's eye chillies, chopped

5 Thai pink shallots or 1 regular, chopped

2 garlic cloves, crushed

2 stalks of lemongrass, trimmed and finely sliced

3 cm fresh ginger, peeled and sliced

1 tablespoon Vietnamese or Thai fish sauce

1 teaspoon ground turmeric

several banana leaves or foil, for wrapping

a steamer or bamboo steamer

Makes 20

Using a sharp knife, cut the fish into 5 x 2 cm pieces, sprinkle with 1 teaspoon of the salt and set aside for 15 minutes.

To make the chilli paste, drain the soaked chillies and put into a small blender. Add the bird's eye chillies, shallots, garlic, lemongrass, ginger, fish sauce and turmeric and blend well. Alternatively, use a mortar and pestle.

Put the eggs into a bowl and beat lightly with a fork. Add the chilli paste and lime leaves and stir well. Stir in the coconut cream and 1 teaspoon of the salt.

Wash and dry the banana leaves, if using. Warm them over an open flame for a few seconds until softened. Cut the leaves or foil into pieces about 18 x 15 cm.

Put a piece of fish into the centre of each piece of leaf or foil. Bring the 2 long sides together, then fold one of the short sides so the centre meets join of the 2 long edges. Fold the corners back and keep together (use a paperclip or plastic clothes peg). Add about 2 tablespoons of the egg mixture to the parcel and fold the other end in the same way. Fasten with a long cocktail stick or piece of bamboo skewer and remove the paperclip or peg. You can also trim the top with scissors to make a neat parcel.

Put the parcels into a steamer set over a saucepan of gently simmering water and steam for 20 minutes, then serve with other Asian dishes.

chinese steamed fish

Chinese cooks are very discerning in choosing their fish – they like a fine textured fish with plenty of flavour for this dish. Grouper was used here, but moonfish, parrotfish or red snapper are also good. Take the lid of the steamer with you when you buy the fish to make sure it will fit.

4–5 Chinese dried mushrooms

1 bundle dried beanthread (cellophane) vermicelli noodles, about 30 g

1 large whole fish, such as grouper or red snapper, about 1 kg, cleaned and scaled

5 cm fresh root ginger, peeled and very finely sliced

3 garlic cloves, crushed

6 spring onions, finely sliced lengthways

1 tablespoon peanut oil for brushing

2 tablespoons soy sauce or Vietnamese or Thai fish sauce

1 teaspoon sugar

2 tablespoons Chinese rice wine (*Shaohsing*), mirin (Japanese rice wine) or dry sherry

an oval serving plate, to fit inside a large steamer

a bamboo or metal steamer

Serves 4

Put the mushrooms into a bowl and pour over enough boiling water to cover. Let soak for 15 minutes. Drain, remove the stems if any, then, using a sharp knife, roughly slice the caps.

Put the serving plate into a large steamer. Put the dried noodles onto the plate, then add the sliced mushrooms.

Rinse the fish in lightly salted water, then pat dry with kitchen paper. Fill the fish cavity with the ginger, garlic and half the spring onions, then brush the skin with the peanut oil. Bring a small saucepan of water to the boil, add the remaining spring onions and blanch for 10 seconds, then drain.

Put the fish onto the oval plate on top of the noodles and mushrooms. Put the soy or fish sauce, sugar and Chinese rice wine into a small bowl, mix quickly, then sprinkle over the fish.

Put the steamer into a wok about one-third full of boiling water. Steam until the flesh has become opaque (the time will depend on the thickness of the fish, but about 20–30 minutes is usual). Add extra boiling water as necessary.

Remove the steamer from the wok, then remove the plate from the steamer. Wipe the underside dry with kitchen paper.

Add the blanched spring onions and serve. (Discard the flavourings from the cavity before serving, but leave the noodles and mushrooms, which will soak up lots of flavour from the juices.)

Note It is regarded as bad luck to turn the fish over. Serve it from one side of the bone, then remove and discard the bones and serve the remaining fish. You can also de-bone the fish before serving, reassembling it carefully on the plate.

green thai fish curry

Thai curries are easy to make, quick to cook and totally delicious. The secret is in the mixture of spices and the freshness of the pastes. You can make the paste in a food processor using ground spices or, if you prefer using whole ones, break them down in a coffee grinder kept solely for that purpose. Store unused paste in the refrigerator.

1 tablespoon peanut oil

400 ml coconut milk

750 g fish fillets, such as monkfish, cod, John Dory or other firm fish

Spice paste

1 onion, sliced

3 garlic cloves, chopped

6 small hot fresh green chillies, deseeded and sliced

5 cm fresh root ginger, peeled and sliced

1 teaspoon ground white pepper

1 teaspoon ground coriander

½ teaspoon ground turmeric

½ teaspoon ground cumin

1 teaspoon shrimp paste (*blachan* or *belacan*), toasted

1 tablespoon Vietnamese or Thai fish sauce

1 stalk of lemongrass, trimmed and finely sliced

To serve

sprigs of fresh Thai basil (optional)

2 limes, halved

fragrant Thai rice or noodles

Serves 4

Put all the spice paste ingredients into a food processor and process until a smooth. Alternatively, use a mortar and pestle. Set aside.

Heat the peanut oil in a wok, add the spice paste and stir-fry for a few seconds to release the aromas. Add the thick portion from the top of the coconut milk, stir well and boil to thicken slightly.

Add the fish and, using a fish slice or spatula, turn the pieces over until they are well coated in the sauce. Reheat to simmering point and cook until they just start to become opaque, about 2 minutes.

Add the remaining coconut milk and continue cooking until the fish is cooked through. Serve topped with Thai basil sprigs, if using, plus the halved limes and fragrant Thai rice or noodles.

Note Thai and Vietnamese basil is quite different from ordinary basil. It is sold in Asian food markets – omit it if you can't find it.

crisp thai noodles
with chillies, pork and prawns

This traditional sweet-but-savoury Thai concoction is amazingly easy to construct, and its garnishes can be added or subtracted according to whatever interesting ingredients you have to hand. However, there are a few ingredients you simply must have: coriander, spring onions, a chilli or two, and a Thai curry paste – this one is the milder orange mussaman (Muslim) paste.

4 bundles rice vermicelli noodles, about 30 g each

peanut oil, for frying

Garnishes

1 tablespoon corn oil

1 tablespoon Thai chilli paste, such as mussaman

4 pork chops, boned and sliced into strips

4–8 uncooked prawns, shelled and split lengthways if large

1–4 fresh chillies, finely sliced

8 spring onions, finely sliced

1 bunch of fresh coriander sprigs

Sweet Thai sauce

125 ml rice vinegar

100 g dark muscovado sugar

4 tablespoons soy sauce

4 tablespoons Vietnamese or Thai fish sauce

Serves 4

To make the Thai sauce, put the vinegar, sugar, soy and fish sauce into a small saucepan and cook, stirring until the sugar has dissolved. Set aside to keep warm.

To prepare the garnishes, heat the oil in a frying pan, add the Thai chilli paste and cook for 1–2 minutes to release the flavours. Add the pork strips and stir-fry until crispy. Add the prawns and stir-fry for 1 minute until opaque. Using a slotted spoon, transfer to a dish and keep warm. Add the chillies and spring onions and stir-fry for 1 minute, then add to the prawns and pork.

To prepare the noodles, line 4 large, warmed serving bowls with kitchen paper, then fill a wok one-third full of corn oil and heat to 190°C (375°F), or until a piece of noodle puffs up immediately. Add a bundle of noodles and fry for 1 minute or until light gold then, using tongs, carefully turn it over and cook the other side. Remove the noodles and put in 1 of the bowls. Repeat with the other 3 bundles (take care to reheat the oil and skim off any debris between batches with a slotted spoon).

When all the bundles are cooked, turn them over in the bowls and discard the paper. Put the pork, prawns, spring onions and chillies on top of the noodles. Pour over the sweet hot dressing, and top with coriander sprigs. Serve.

meat & poultry

Asian cooks are endlessly inventive and insist on top quality, fresh ingredients. Chicken, duck, pork and occasionally beef are used, sometimes separately, often together, and even more often cooked with shrimp and other seafood.

bangkok chicken

This classic green Thai curry is based on a recipe from the renowned Oriental Hotel in Bangkok. Curries like these are served with a selection of other dishes, such as steamed rice, plain beanthread noodles and one or more vegetable dishes. Thai cooks would use incendiary amounts of chillies, often the tiny, blindingly hot, bird's eye chillies, but for Western palates the quantity has been reduced. Spice pastes – red, green, orange mussaman and so on – are an intrinsic part of Thai cooking. This paste makes double the amount you'll need, so you'll have extra to use in other dishes. You can also buy ready-made paste.

2 tablespoons peanut oil

4 skinless chicken breasts, about 800 g, quartered crossways

150 ml chicken stock

500 ml canned coconut milk

125 g Thai 'pea' aubergines or chopped cucumber

1 teaspoon Vietnamese or Thai fish sauce or 1 teaspoon salt

freshly squeezed juice of 1 lime

a large bunch of fresh Thai basil or mint

boiled fragrant Thai rice, to serve

Green curry paste

5–6 fresh green chillies, deseeded and sliced

1 small bunch of fresh coriander, chopped

2 stalks of fresh lemongrass, trimmed and finely sliced

3 cm fresh ginger, peeled and finely sliced

3 cm fresh galangal, peeled and sliced (optional)

4 fresh kaffir lime leaves, shredded hair-thin

2 teaspoons coriander seeds, crushed

1 teaspoon cumin seeds, crushed

4 spring onions or small red onions, chopped

4 garlic cloves, crushed

Serves 4

Put all the green curry paste ingredients into a food processor and process until smooth. Alternatively, use a mortar and pestle. Set aside half the mixture for this recipe and refrigerate or freeze the rest.

Heat the peanut oil in a large, preferably non-stick, frying pan or wok, add the chicken and sauté for 2–3 minutes or until firm and golden. Using tongs, turn the pieces over as they cook.

Stir in the reserved green curry paste and sauté, stirring constantly, for about 1 minute. Add the chicken stock and bring to the boil.

Add half the coconut milk and the 'pea' aubergines or cucumber and cook, covered, at a rapid simmer (not a boil) for 5 minutes. Using tongs, turn the chicken pieces over, then reduce the heat to a very gentle simmer. Add the remaining coconut milk and the fish sauce or salt and cook, uncovered, for a further 8–12 minutes.

Add the lime juice and sprinkle with Thai basil or mint. Transfer to 4 soup bowls and serve immediately with fragrant Thai rice.

Almost all the world appreciates this dish, though few people stir-fry at the hot, fierce temperatures the Chinese do. Stir-fried also means 'steam-stirred' since the tender vegetables mostly cook in the aromatic steam. Use a sweet chilli sauce, not a fiery Thai version or Indonesian sambal: this is a dish from China, after all.

stir-fried chicken with greens

2 tablespoons peanut oil

500 g chicken breasts, cubed, or 3 large skinless, boneless breasts cut into 5 cm strips or cubes

5 cm fresh ginger, peeled and shredded

2 garlic cloves, sliced

250 g broccoli, broken into tiny florets

8 spring onions, halved crossways

175 g green beans, halved and blanched in boiling salted water

1 red or yellow pepper, deseeded and cut into strips

6 tablespoons chicken stock or water

2 tablespoons sweet chilli sauce

1 tablespoon light soy sauce

50 g mangetout, trimmed and washed

50 g sugar snap peas, trimmed and washed

100 g baby bok choy leaves, trimmed and washed

boiled noodles or rice, to serve

Serves 4

Put the peanut oil into a wok and heat until very hot but not smoking. Alternatively, use a large, preferably non-stick, frying pan. Add the chicken and stir-fry over high heat for 2 minutes, then add the ginger and garlic and stir-fry for a further 2 minutes.

Add the prepared broccoli, spring onions, green beans, sliced pepper and chicken stock or water. Cover and cook for a further 2–3 minutes. Stir in the chilli sauce and soy sauce. Toss the still-wet mangetout, sugar snap peas and bok choy leaves on top. Cover and cook for 1–2 minutes. Toss well and transfer to 4 serving bowls. Serve while the tastes and colours are still vivid and textures crisp with noodles or rice.

hunan chicken

Hunan is the centre of a distinctive, northern school of cooking with a number of crisp but flavourful dishes. This chicken dish is one of the most famous. First the spicy marinade flavours the chicken, then a light, crisp crust forms outside it and acts as a delicious contrast.

6 chicken thighs

6 chicken drumsticks

50 g cornflour

peanut oil, for frying

Marinade

1 tablespoon Szechuan peppercorns, pan-toasted for 1 minute

1 tablespoon caster sugar

5 cm fresh ginger, peeled and grated

4 spring onions, finely chopped

2 tablespoons soy sauce

Dipping sauce

4 tablespoons black bean sauce

2 tablespoons sweet chilli sauce

125 ml tomato passata or juice

2 tablespoons light soy sauce

2 spring onions, finely shredded, and green ends reserved for serving

a large heavy-based saucepan or deep-fryer

Serves 4

Rinse the chicken under cold running water and pat dry with kitchen paper. Prick each piece several times with a fork, to let the marinade penetrate well.

To make the marinade, put the toasted Szechuan peppercorns, sugar, ginger, spring onions and soy sauce into a food processor and process until smooth. Alternatively, use a mortar and pestle. Transfer the mixture to a large plastic bag, then add the chicken pieces and turn to coat. Using your hands, massage in the marinade, then press out any excess air, seal tightly and chill in the refrigerator for 1 hour.

To make the dipping sauce, put all the ingredients into a small bowl and mix well. Transfer to 4 small dipping bowls and set aside.

Put the cornflour into a large, shallow dish. Drain the chicken, then roll each piece in the cornflour to coat.

Pour 7.5 cm depth of peanut oil into a heavy-based saucepan or deep-fryer and heat to 190°C (375°F), or until a piece of noodle puffs up immediately. Using tongs, add the chicken pieces in batches of 4–6. Deep-fry for 7–8 minutes on each side. Test if the chicken is cooked – the flesh must be totally opaque and firm, right through to the bone. Remove and drain on crumpled kitchen paper, keeping the pieces warm in the oven while you cook the remaining chicken pieces.

Transfer to 4 large bowls and serve with chopsticks and the small bowls of dipping sauce, topped with green spring onion shreds.

In this easy, minimal, but classic Japanese dish, sake is used to add sweetness and flavour and act as a tenderizer. Salt adds balance to the taste. These breasts are often skewered with three bamboo satay sticks in the shape of a fan: it stabilizes them for even cooking, but also looks elegant. Do not overcook this chicken: 12 minutes at the most.

japanese salt-grilled chicken

4 boneless, skinless chicken breasts

3 tablespoons sake or dry sherry

sea salt flakes

To serve

4 spring onions

Japanese pink pickled ginger

12 bamboo satay sticks, soaked in water for 30 minutes

Serves 4

Put each chicken breast between 2 sheets of foil. Using your hand, a meat mallet or a rolling pin, pound and flatten them to about half the original thickness. Transfer to a glass or ceramic dish and pour over the sake, turn the chicken to coat and set aside for about 5–10 minutes to tenderize.

Remove the chicken from the dish and push 3 bamboo satay sticks through the length of each breast to hold them flat.

Sprinkle a layer of salt over both sides of each piece of chicken. Put each piece onto a sheet of foil and cook under a preheated hot grill or over hot coals on a barbecue for 4–5 minutes, about 5 cm from the heat. Turn the chicken over and cook for a further 2–4 minutes. The chicken must be golden brown, cooked right through, but not dry.

Eat hot, warm or cold with a spring onion and a pile of pink pickled ginger.

A famous and princely dish. Though easily available these days ready prepared from many Chinese restaurants, it is fascinating to know how to make the duck yourself. A hair dryer or electric fan is useful if you do not live in a place with a hot, dry, windy climate (in other words, most of us). Most often served with pancakes and garnishes, the duck is also excellent with plain rice. Try it, adding the cucumber, spring onion and plum sauce as accompaniments. Serve soup made from the carcass later.

peking duck

1 plump duck, about 1.5 kg, cleaned and prepared

1 teaspoon Chinese five-spice powder

2 teaspoons salt

2 tablespoons Chinese oyster sauce

peanut oil, for frying

Glaze

2 tablespoons golden syrup

2 teaspoons distilled white malt vinegar

2 teaspoons sake or vodka

To serve

1 kg cooked rice or 16 Peking duck pancakes

20 cm cucumber, cut into 5 cm strips

8 spring onions, finely sliced lengthways

250 ml plum sauce (page 37) or hoisin sauce

Serves 4

Wash the duck well under cold running water and pat dry on kitchen paper. Put the Chinese five-spice, salt and oyster sauce into a bowl and mix well. Rub it all over the inside of the bird, then tie a long string around the neck and neck skin so the duck can be hung up. Put the duck into a colander and pour boiling water over it 5 times, letting the bird dry off between each pouring. Pat dry again.

Put the glaze ingredients into a small saucepan with 125 ml water, bring to the boil and cook until sticky, about 10 minutes. Using a small brush, paint the glaze all over the duck. Hang up the bird by the string in a hot, breezy place or in front of a hair dryer or electric fan, until it is completely dry.

Fill a large wok or frying pan one-third full of peanut oil and heat to 190°C (375°F), or until a piece of noodle puffs up immediately. Using tongs, add the duck and deep-fry for 30 minutes, then turn over and deep-fry for a further 30 minutes.

Alternatively, put the duck on its back on a rack in a roasting tin and cook in a preheated oven at 190°C (375°F) Gas 5 for 45 minutes. Reduce the temperature to 150°C (300°F) Gas 2, turn the duck onto its breast and roast for 30 minutes. Increase the temperature to 190°C (375°F) Gas 5, turn the duck over again and roast for a further 30 minutes.

To serve, slice the duck, including skin, meat and bones, into 1 cm slices with a Chinese cleaver or heavy sharp knife. Transfer to a serving plate and serve hot with rice or pancakes, cucumber, spring onions and plum or hoisin sauce.

A delicious recipe from the border of China and former Indochina – the tang of orange mixed with crushed yellow bean sauce is definitely a gorgeous combination and the whole dish can be easily prepared in advance up to the point where it is transferred to the oven. A word of warning – the sauce around the duck must be very thick before it is put into the oven, because the bok choy or cabbage gives off so much water that the dish can easily become diluted.

braised duck and ginger

4 large duck breasts, cut into thick slices

5 teaspoons cornflour

4 tablespoons yellow bean paste or sauce

2 tablespoons Chinese rice wine (*Shaohsing*), mirin (Japanese rice wine) or dry sherry

2 teaspoons sugar

1 onion, finely chopped

2 tablespoons peanut oil

10 cm fresh ginger, peeled and thickly sliced

2 garlic cloves, crushed

zest of 1 orange or 1 tangerine

2 tablespoons dark soy sauce

4 baby bok choy, halved lengthways, or ½ Chinese cabbage, sliced crossways

freshly ground black pepper

4 spring onions, sliced, to serve

a Chinese sandpot or deep casserole dish

Serves 4

Put the duck into a large bowl, sprinkle with 1 teaspoon of the cornflour and mix until the duck slices are coated all over.

Heat a wok or frying pan, add the duck (without adding any oil) and stir-fry to release the fat and firm up the meat. Remove with a slotted spoon and return the duck to the bowl.

Put the bean paste or sauce into a small bowl, add 125 ml water, the Chinese rice wine or mirin, sugar and freshly ground black pepper, and mix well.

Add the onion to the wok or pan, then add the bean paste mixture. Simmer for about 30 seconds, then pour the mixture over the duck. Reheat the wok with the peanut oil, add the ginger and garlic and sauté to release their flavours. Return the duck and its sauce to the wok or pan, add the orange zest and simmer lightly until most of the water has evaporated.

Mix the remaining cornflour with 2 tablespoons of water and the soy sauce in a small bowl. Stir into the wok and bring to the boil, stirring constantly.

Line a Chinese sandpot or casserole with the bok choy or Chinese cabbage, arrange the duck over the top, then pour over the sauce and cook in a preheated oven at 180°C (350°F) Gas 4 for 10 minutes until tender. Remove from the oven and, if the leaves have given off too much liquid, pour the sauce into a saucepan or wok and boil until it thickens again to a coating consistency. Return to the pot, sprinkle with the spring onions and serve with other Chinese dishes.

'Red-cooking' is a Chinese braising method for whole ducks, chickens, or large pieces of pork – and the red colour comes from soy sauce. This dish uses a great deal of soy, but the stock can be used again and again (freeze between uses). Use dark soy, which is less salty than light.

red-cooked pork

1 kg pork spareribs, loin or shoulder, in the piece

Red stock

500 ml Chinese rice wine (*Shaohsing*)

750 ml chicken stock or water

500 ml dark soy sauce

2 tablespoons rice vinegar

2 cinnamon sticks

3 cm fresh ginger, peeled and sliced

zest of 1 tangerine or orange

2 whole star anise

6 spring onions

noodles, rice or stir-fried vegetables, to serve

a large flameproof casserole dish

Serves 6–8

Put all the stock ingredients into a large flameproof casserole dish and bring to the boil. Add the pork, return to the boil, then simmer on top of the stove or in a preheated oven at 180°C (350°F) Gas 4 for 45 minutes if using pork loin, or 1½ hours if using pork shoulder or spareribs. When the meat is very tender, carefully lift it out onto on a wooden board and, using a Chinese cleaver or heavy knife, cut it into thick slices or bite-sized chunks. Serve a little of the stock, plus other Chinese dishes such as noodles, stir-fried vegetables or steamed rice.

Note Some of the stock is served with the dish, the rest is kept and used over and over again, improving in flavour each time a new dish is cooked in it – if you don't plan to make this often, the stock may be frozen.

Variations

For extra flavour, marinate the pork overnight in the refrigerator in a South-east Asian spice paste. Put 1 teaspoon ground coriander, 1 teaspoon crushed white peppercorns, 4 crushed garlic cloves, 2 stalks of lemongrass, trimmed and chopped, 5 cm fresh ginger, peeled and chopped, 4 fresh red chillies, deseeded and chopped, 2 teaspoons shrimp paste (*blachan* or *belacan*) optional, 1 tablespoon sunflower oil and 2 teaspoons rice vinegar into a blender and process until a smooth paste forms. Alternatively, use a mortar and pestle. Spread the mixture over the pork and marinate overnight in the refrigerator.

Although red-cooked pork is a typical Chinese dish – and perfect served with other Chinese dishes – it is also delicious served with mashed potatoes or mashed white beans, with a little of the stock drizzled over.

deep-fried chilli beef

300–350 g beef rump steak, fillet or entrecôte, cut 1.5 cm thick

1 tablespoon dark soy sauce

2–3 tablespoons hot chilli sauce

1 small fresh hot chilli, deseeded and chopped

2 tablespoons Chinese rice wine (*Shaohsing*) or dry sherry

2 tablespoons cornflour

1 tablespoon chilli oil or peanut oil

250 g broccoli

1 medium carrot

175 g fresh shiitake, chestnut or large open mushrooms (optional)

2.5 cm fresh ginger, peeled and finely sliced

250 g canned bamboo shoots, drained

1 teaspoon sugar

1 teaspoon sea salt flakes

4 tablespoons beef stock or beer

4 spring onions, finely sliced (optional)

peanut oil, for frying

Serves 4

Beef has always been a rare and prized ingredient in China. However, in the West, where it is widely available, this is one of the best-known Chinese beef dishes. The cut used here is a thick, tender steak of rump, fillet or entrecôte, but you can experiment with cheaper, less tender but highly flavoured cuts such as flank, blade or skirt. Cut it thinly and tenderize it in the Chinese way, by marinating it in a mixture of water and baking soda, or in the Western way, with a few teaspoons of vinegar. Rub into the meat before the other flavourings.

To make the beef easier to cut, half-freeze it until firm. Using a Chinese cleaver or other very sharp knife, slice it into wafer-thin strips, across the grain or on the diagonal. Cut these slices crossways into 2–3 pieces.

Put the soy sauce, chilli sauce, chilli, Chinese rice wine and cornflour into a small bowl and mix together. Add the beef strips, toss until well coated, then sprinkle with 1 tablespoon of the chilli or peanut oil and set aside.

To prepare the vegetables, separate the broccoli into small florets and cut the carrot diagonally into thick slices. If using mushrooms, remove and discard the shiitake stems, and cut the larger mushrooms into halves or quarters.

Fill a wok about one-third full of peanut oil and heat to 190°C (375°F), or until a piece of noodle puffs up immediately. Add the beef and deep-fry rapidly for 15–30 seconds or until brown outside, part-rare inside. Remove with a slotted spoon and drain on crumpled kitchen paper. Keep the beef warm.

Pour off most of the oil, leaving about 4 tablespoons in the wok. Add the ginger and carrots and stir-fry for 1 minute, then add the broccoli, bamboo shoots and mushrooms, if using, and stir-fry for 1 minute until crisp and tender. Add the sugar, salt and stock or beer, then return the beef to the wok. Reheat briefly, stirring constantly, then serve, sprinkled with sliced spring onions, if using.

1 kg boneless pork loin

1 tablespoon coriander seeds

½ teaspoon ground turmeric

1 teaspoon salt

1 tablespoon brown sugar

1 stalk of lemongrass, trimmed and finely sliced

5 small shallots, finely chopped

125 ml sunflower or peanut oil

1 cucumber, quartered lengthways, deseeded, then sliced crossways

dipping sauce such as soy sauce or *nuóc cham* (page 17), to serve

20 bamboo skewers, soaked in water for at least 30 minutes

Makes 20

Using a sharp knife, cut the pork into 2 cm slices, then cut each slice into 2 cm cubes and set aside.

Put the coriander seeds into a dry frying pan and heat until aromatic. Using a mortar and pestle, grind to a powder. Alternatively, use a spice grinder or clean coffee grinder. Transfer to a wide bowl, then add the turmeric, salt and sugar.

Put the finely sliced lemongrass and shallots into a spice grinder or blender and process until smooth (add a little water, if necessary). Add to the bowl and stir well. Stir in 2 tablespoons of the sunflower oil.

Add the cubes of meat and toss to coat with the mixture. Cover and set aside to marinate in the refrigerator for 2 hours or overnight.

Thread 2 pieces of pork onto each soaked wooden skewer and brush with the remaining sunflower oil. Cook under a preheated hot grill or over medium hot coals on a barbecue until cooked. Thread a piece of cucumber onto the end of each skewer and serve with the dipping sauce.

singapore pork satays

Aromatic skewers of meat, fish, vegetables and poultry are ubiquitous street food all over South-east Asia – and popular starters in restaurants too. They are easy to make – great for a party and delicious as part of your barbecue repertoire. These satays are served with a Chinese soy sauce dip, or a South-east Asian influenced sauce made with fish sauce or peanuts.

500 g beef steak

125 ml coconut milk

grated zest and juice of 2 limes

2 fresh red chillies, finely chopped

3 stalks of lemongrass,
trimmed and finely chopped

3 garlic cloves, crushed

1 teaspoon ground cumin

2 teaspoons ground coriander

1 teaspoon ground cardamom

2 tablespoons Vietnamese or Thai fish sauce,
or soy sauce

1 teaspoon sugar

sunflower or peanut oil, for brushing

dipping sauce, such as soy sauce
or *nuóc cham* (page 17), to serve

*10 bamboo skewers, soaked in water
for at least 30 minutes*

Makes about 10

Using a sharp knife, cut the beef crossways into thin strips, about 5 mm thick and 5 cm long. Put the coconut milk, lime zest and juice, chillies, lemongrass, garlic, cumin, coriander and cardamom into a bowl, then stir in fish sauce or soy sauce and sugar. Add the beef strips and toss to coat. Cover and chill in the refrigerator for 2 hours or overnight to develop the flavours.

Drain the beef, discarding the marinade. Thread the beef in a zig-zag pattern onto the presoaked skewers and cook under a preheated hot grill or in a frying pan (brushed with a film of peanut oil) until browned and tender. Serve on a platter with a small bowl of dipping sauce.

indonesian beef satays

Satay sauce, made with peanuts, is common in many parts of South-east Asia, but especially in Indonesia. You can also make up these skewers with other meats, such as chicken, duck or pork, and they will be equally delicious.

sweet **things**

Asians have a fierce sweet tooth and consume sweet things almost constantly, though not at the end of a meal. Chinese cake shops are full of custard tarts and tooth-tingling sweetmeats, while Thai and Vietnamese street vendors do a roaring trade in smoothies, juices and spicy cooked fruits.

orange and almond fortune cookies

The Westernized version of the fortune cookie – found all around the world – is good fun, but is always a bland, tough thing. The cookie in this recipe is light, crisp and delicious, and can be wrapped around the fortune of your choice, from the traditional to the hilarious or the personal.

2 egg whites

75 g caster sugar

50 g ground almonds

50 g plain flour, sifted

50 g butter, melted and cooled

1 teaspoon orange flower water (optional)

finely grated zest of 1 orange

a baking sheet, lined with baking parchment

24 small pieces of paper with fortunes

Makes 24

Put the egg whites into a spotlessly clean, greasefree bowl and, using an electric mixer or balloon whisk, whisk until very stiff. Gently fold in the sugar, almonds, flour, cooled butter, orange flower water, if using, and orange zest.

Spread teaspoons of the mixture very thinly onto the prepared baking sheet, spaced well apart (4–6 should fit on the sheet). Bake in a preheated oven at 190°C (375°F) Gas 5 for 6–8 minutes until golden. Working very quickly, fold each cookie in half around a fortune. Let cool on a wire rack. Repeat until all the cookies are made.

The cookies will keep for up to 1 week in an airtight container.

Many people end a celebration meal at a Chinese restaurant with this simple but superb treat. It is worth learning to do it well, so choose flavourful, crisp apples. You can arrange this dish so everyone dips their own apple pieces into the caramel – have all the ingredients prepared and on the table, together with bowls of iced water to set the toffee. Alternatively, for a more sober presentation, prepare the dish ahead and take it to the table complete, as here.

chinese toffee apples

4 sweet apples, such as Cox's, Gala or Braeburn

6 tablespoons plain flour

1 tablespoon cornflour or rice flour

2 egg whites, beaten to a froth

125 g caster sugar

2 tablespoons white sesame seeds or black sesame seeds

peanut or sunflower oil, for frying

a bowl of iced water, for setting toffee

Serves 4

Using a sharp knife, peel and core the apples and cut each one into 4, 6 or 8 pieces depending on size. Roll in 2 tablespoons of the plain flour to coat well.

Put the remaining plain flour, cornflour or rice flour and egg whites into a bowl and, using an electric mixer or whisk, whisk to form a light batter.

Fill a wok one-third full of peanut oil and heat to 190°C (375°F), or until a piece of noodle puffs up immediately. Dip each piece of apple into the batter and, using a slotted spoon, lower carefully into the hot oil. Deep-fry in batches for 3 minutes each, then remove and drain on kitchen paper.

Put the sugar and 2 tablespoons of water into a small saucepan and heat until dissolved. Add 1 tablespoon of the oil, then increase the heat to high and cook, stirring with chopsticks occasionally, until a golden-red toffee or caramel forms. Turn off the heat.

Dip each piece of deep-fried apple into the caramel (as it darkens and thickens, it will cling better to the battered surface), then sprinkle each piece with sesame seeds. Dip briefly in iced water to set the toffee, then serve.

five-spice custard tarts

Chinese five-spice powder can be a combination of many spices – Szechuan pepper, cinnamon, cloves, fennel, star anise, cassia, liquorice root – all mixed to add flavour to savoury dishes. Here, a careful selection of spices makes a wonderful addition to sweet custard tarts, served throughout a dim sum (*yum cha*) meal.

350 g sweet shortcrust pastry

250 ml milk

250 ml double cream

1 cinnamon stick

4 whole star anise

6 whole cloves

6 pieces of liquorice root (optional)

4 eggs

50 g sugar

1 whole nutmeg

8 cm biscuit cutter, plain or fluted

small tart trays (12 hole) or 24 mini brioche tins, greased

Makes 24

Put the pastry onto a board and roll out to 2 mm thickness. Cut out 24 circles with the biscuit cutter and use to line the prepared trays or tins. Chill in the refrigerator for about 30 minutes.

Put the milk and cream into a small saucepan and slowly bring to the boil. Add the cinnamon, star anise, cloves and liquorice root, if using. Remove from the heat and let infuse for 30 minutes.

Put the eggs and sugar into a bowl and, using an electric mixer or balloon whisk, whisk until pale. Pour in the milk mixture through a sieve and whisk.

Pour the filling into the pastry cases and grate a little nutmeg on top. Bake in a preheated oven at 180°C (350°F) Gas 4 for 15–20 minutes until the custard has set. Remove from the oven and let cool, then serve.

In Cambodia, sticky rice is cooked in a woven bamboo basket steamer set over a pot a little like a couscoussière. There is a Vietnamese old wives' tale that if you don't look after your stomach, when you get old, you'll have to eat sticky rice – so presumably it's easy to digest.

sticky rice with mango

250 ml sticky rice

2 ripe mangoes

250 ml canned coconut milk

4 tablespoons white sugar

a small pinch of salt

a steamer lined with muslin or presoaked bamboo rice steamer

Serves 4

Put the sticky rice into a bowl and rinse, changing the water several times, until the water runs clear. Cover the rice with cold water and transfer to the refrigerator and let soak overnight.

When ready to cook, drain the rice and put into a prepared steamer or bamboo rice steamer. Cover and steam for about 45 minutes or until done. Remove from the heat and fluff up the rice with a fork.

Meanwhile, to prepare the mangoes, cut the cheeks off either side of the seed with a sharp knife, then cut a chequerboard into the flesh without going through the skin. Lift off the pieces of mango with a fork. Peel the remaining skin off the mango and dice the remaining flesh (or eat as the cook's treat).

Transfer the cooked rice to a saucepan, add the coconut milk, sugar and salt, and cook until the sugar has dissolved and the rice is thick. Serve in bowls, topped with the mango.

Note It is traditional to chill the mango, but the fruit has more flavour at room temperature. Also, never put fruit into the refrigerator for more than 30 minutes or so – if they're tropicals, you'll give them frostbite!

Variation

Sticky Rice Cake with Palm Sugar Syrup Spoon the cooked sticky rice into a non-stick springform cake tin and let set. Don't refrigerate (it can be left in the tin for several hours). To make the syrup, dissolve about 4 tablespoons of brown sugar in 4 tablespoons hot water. To serve, remove the cake from the tin, cut into wedges and put onto serving plates. Drizzle the sugar syrup over the top and serve with mango.

Black rice in coconut milk is a traditional South-east Asian sweet dish. It is even more delicious teamed with red fruits. Cherries and raspberries aren't tropical fruits, however, so feel free to use alternatives such as papaya or lychees.

black rice with red fruits

250 ml Asian black rice

red fruits, such as cherries, halved and pitted, or raspberries, to serve

Coconut ginger syrup

500 ml canned coconut cream

4 tablespoons brown sugar

3 cm fresh ginger, peeled and grated

a pinch of salt

a steamer lined with muslin or presoaked bamboo rice steamer

Serves 4

Put the black rice into a large bowl and pour over enough cold water to cover. Let soak for at least 4 hours, or overnight in the refrigerator.

When ready to cook the rice, drain, then put the rice into a prepared steamer or bamboo rice steamer. Cover and steam for about 1 hour or until tender. Remove from the heat and fluff up the rice with a fork.

To make the sauce, put the coconut cream into a small saucepan, add the sugar, ginger and salt, then bring to the boil and cook until the sugar has dissolved.

Add the cooked rice to the pan and simmer until thick. Let cool but do not chill. When cool, serve topped with the fruit.

watermelon and lime smoothie

All over South-east Asia, food markets, hole-in-the-wall juice bars and street vendors sell all kinds of fresh juices; watermelon, pineapple, orange, sugar cane, and tropical fruits you sometimes can't even recognize. The street vendors push little glass-topped carts with ready-sliced fruit kept cold ready for squeezing or blending. The fruit always seems better than at home: they have always ripened on the tree or plant, and have flavor and colour you just can't imagine. And remember, the smoothie is a traditional drink in Vietnam and Thailand, and was taken to the States and Australia by returning troops.

red flesh from 1 round watermelon, deseeded

3 cm fresh ginger, peeled and grated

sugar, to taste

To serve

crushed ice

2 limes, cut into wedges

Serves 4

Press the melon flesh and ginger through a juicer or put into a blender and purée until smooth. If using a blender, you may need to add ice cubes and a little water to let the blades run.

Add sugar to taste, then pour into a jug half filled with crushed ice. Serve immediately in glasses with lime wedges for squeezing.

Variation

In South-east Asia, smoothies are thickened with sweetened condensed milk, which makes them delicious and creamy – just a dollop or two is needed. If you use condensed milk, you may not need sugar, so taste and test before adding any sweetener.

mango and coconut milk

There are something like six hundred varieties of mangoes in Asia – some are sweet and eaten as fresh fruit, or chopped and served with sweet sticky rice. Others are very soft and known as 'sucking mangoes'. These you squash between your fingers until soft, then stick a hole in one end and suck out the sweet juice. Still others are used green – grated in salads, or cooked in dishes as a souring agent, rather like lemon juice. The green ones are also used to make spicy pickles. Use the sweet ones to make drinks, and let them get really ripe first. Alternatively, in Indian stores, you can buy cans of Alphonso mango purée, made from the best-tasting mangoes in the world. You can also add cream and churn into ice cream or serve chilled as a fool.

2 fresh ripe mangoes, peeled and flesh cut off the seed, or 250 ml canned mango purée

juice of ½ lime

250 ml desiccated coconut (measured by volume), or canned coconut milk (optional)

Serves 2

Put the mangoes, lime juice and coconut milk into a blender and process until smooth. Transfer to a jug and chill in the refrigerator.

If using desiccated coconut, put it into a blender with 250 ml iced water. Blend until frothy. Let stand for 5 minutes, then blend again. Strain into the jug and return the coconut to the blender. Repeat with another 250 ml iced water. Strain, then stir into the jug of mango and lime or lemon and discard the soaked coconut. Serve immediately. Alternatively, omit the coconut milk and just blend the mango and lime or lemon juice with enough ice cubes and water to make a pourable consistency.

the basics: rice

Measuring Rice and Water

The easiest method is by volume: take one container of rice and add multiples of that container of hot water or stock; 1 plus 15 per cent for sushi rice, 2 for most other kinds of rice. Bring to the boil, cover the saucepan, reduce the heat and simmer until done – usually, though not always, 12 minutes.

Absorption method: put the rice into a large saucepan and pour over enough liquid to cover, to a depth of one finger joint above the rice. Bring to the boil, cover, reduce the heat and simmer until done (usually 12 minutes).

Electric Rice Cooker

These convenient, fool-proof machines make cooking rice child's play. You should follow the instructions given with each machine, but the usual method is to measure the rice, then add the level of water relevant to that type. Add no salt. Cover and switch on. When the rice is done, the machine turns off automatically and the rice will keep hot for up to 1 hour. (After that it will begin to deteriorate.) Perfect for families who eat at different times, though some cooks think this method is somewhat impersonal. Glutinous rice can also be cooked this way, though it takes longer – a microwave is a good alternative.

Steamed Rice

When Asian cooks or restaurants specify 'steamed rice', unless they're using sticky rice (see below), they may well mean rice cooked in boiling water and steam by the absorption method or even in an electric rice cooker.

Sticky Rice

Put the rice into a bowl and rinse, changing the water several times, until the water runs clear. Cover the rice with cold water, put into the refrigerator and let soak overnight. When ready to cook, drain the rice, then line a steamer with muslin or prepare a soaked bamboo steamer (see right). Cover and steam for about 45 minutes until done. Remove from the heat and fluff up with a fork.

rice varieties

White Long Grain

(Texmati, Carolina, Patna, etc.)
Long grain, white, milled, not glutinous.
Comments: Mainly savoury use. Easily absorbs double its volume of liquid. Useful all-purpose rice but needs assertive seasoning and accompaniments. A favourite all-purpose and everyday rice in the West. Many varieties available. Grains are separate when cooked.
Sources: Grocers, supermarkets, delicatessens.
Cooking and timing: 12–15 minutes or follow packet instructions. Cooking methods; pan-of-water, absorption, rice cooker or microwave.

Black Glutinous Rice

(Black sweet rice, wild sweet rice)
Short to medium grain. Actually garnet red, not black. Milled. Red colour only in outer layer of milled grain. Glutinous. *Note:* glutinous rice does not contain gluten.
Comments: Rich, earthy flavour. Combines well with coconut sugar, other palm sugars, coconut milk and pandanus. Usually used in sweet dishes. Not a staple except in Laos, Vietnam, Cambodia and Thailand. Only 2 per cent of the world harvest is glutinous (sticky) rice.
Sources: Asian grocers and supermarkets, specialist delicatessens.
Cooking and timing: 25–30 minutes. (Beware: colour 'dyes' other foods present.) Cooking methods; absorption, additional liquids as listed in recipe, rice cooker or microwave.

Thai Fragrant Rice

(Jasmine rice, sweet rice)
Long grain. White, milled. Slightly sticky (glutinous). Note: glutinous rice does not contain gluten.
Comments: Mainly savoury use. The favourite everyday rice of Thai and South-east Asian cooks. Authentic flavour for a large range of South-east Asian dishes. Slight stickiness makes it perfect for Western as well as Eastern palates. Good with Thai-style curries or stir-fries. Some people rinse cooked rice briefly under boiling water to separate clumps.
Sources: Asian grocers and supermarkets, specialist supermarkets, delicatessens.
Cooking and timing: 12–15 minutes, 25 minutes if cooked in a double-boiler, or follow the packet instructions. *Cooking methods;* double boiler, absorption, pan-of-water, rice cooker or microwave.

Japanese Sushi Rice

(Japanese sweet rice, Japanese medium grain rice, Japanese sticky rice, Korean rice, Kokuho rose)
Plump, short grain. White, milled. Glutinous.

Note: glutinous rice does not contain gluten.
Comments: Sticky, absorbent, perfect for sushi where grains must stick together. Expensive, high quality, needs less water than other types. Take care to avoid sticking.
Sources: Japanese supermarkets, delicatessens, Asian grocers, specialist supermarkets.
Cooking and timing: 15–20 minutes plus standing time, or follow the packet instructions.
Cooking methods; absorption, rice cooker or microwave.

Thai red rice

(Similar to European Camargue red rice)
In general, coloured rice is not as highly regarded in Asia as polished white rice.
Oval, medium grain. Brownish red colour. Milled not hulled. Earthy taste, chewy, firm texture, like other red rice, tipped to be a future culinary star in the West.
Cooking and timing: 30–45 minutes, or follow packet instructions. Cooking methods: pan-of-water, absorption method, pressure cooker, microwave.

South-east Asian Sticky Rice

Sticky rice is the glutinous variety used in Lao, Thai and Vietnamese cooking, especially for sweet dishes.
If you have access to a South-east Asian shop, you may be able to buy the conical woven bamboo rice steamers used in Cambodia. The bamboo, which should be properly soaked before use, is said to give a special flavour to the sticky rice, much appreciated by aficionados.
Cooking and timing: Should always be steamed (see method left), about 45 minutes.

other rice products

Sake

(Japanese rice wine)
Pale to deep gold. Sherry, diluted gin or vodka, dry vermouth or Chinese rice wine can be substituted. Two grades available – one for cooking and one for drinking. Usually drunk warm.
Sources: Specialist grocers or supermarkets.
Cooking and timing: Use in batters, marinades, dressings, sauces. To serve as a beverage, heat gently over hot water.

Mirin (Japanese sweetened rice wine) and **Shaohsing** (Chinese sweetened rice wine)
Clear pale yellow liquid, more diluted than sake. If unavailable, substitute as sake.
Sources: As sake.
Cooking and timing: Used in cooked rice, dressings.

Rice Vinegar

(Red, Clear white, Yellow or Black rice vinegar)
Used in dressings, marinades, sauces, dips and rice dishes. Red is mellow, fruity, (almost like balsamic vinegar) with decisive flavour. Clear white is sharp, yellow is mellow, black tastes caramelized.
Sources: Asian grocers, specialist supermarkets.

Mochi Cakes

Hard, dry blocks of cooked glutinous rice. Not to be confused with fresh mochi cakes which are a ready-to-eat snack.
Sources: Japanese shops, Asian markets.
Cooking and timing: Soften 5–15 minutes in very hot water. Drain then grill or poach. Use in composite dishes such as soups or casseroles.

Ground Rice

Coarse to medium ground meal. In South-east Asia, it is toasted and added to some meat dishes. Used to make desserts, batters, milk puddings, crisp doughs.
Comments: Useful thickener, but glutinous rice flour better for fine biscuits, doughs, batters, wrappers.
Sources: Grocers, supermarkets.
Cooking and timing: Generally 50 g added to 600 ml of hot liquid. Cooks in 10–15 minutes.

Rice Flour

Fine flour used for thickening, and to give lightness to sauces, batters and doughs. Use instead of potato or cornflour in certain dishes.
Sources: Supermarkets, delicatessens.
Cooking and timing: Used in doughs, mixtures.

Flaked Rice

Young rice, used as a coating for fried foods in Asia. In the West, used for puddings, cereals, quick cooking and thickening in hot liquid.
Sources: Some supermarkets.
Cooking and timing: cook 40 g in 600 ml hot milk 10–12 minutes, until thick and creamy.

Rice Crackers

Proprietary snack food, low-calorie, gluten-free.
Sources: Supermarkets, wholefood shops.

Ricepaper

Used under baked items (not made of true rice, but of the pith of an Asian tree).
Sources: Cake-making shops, supermarkets.
Cooking and timing: Edible, needs no cooking.
(See also Ricepaper Wrappers, page 139)

Rice Noodles

See page 138.

the basics: noodles

Noodles are sold fresh or dried. Fresh ones are sold in Asian stores: dried ones are common and many are available in supermarkets and healthfood shops. Some are rare outside their country of origin, but are listed here for interest. Noodles are a sign of Chinese influence and are always eaten with chopsticks, even in countries such as Thailand where chopsticks aren't used for any other food. Fresh noodles are already cooked, so need a very short reheating time, no more than fresh pasta. When dried noodles are soaked in water before use, the dry weight will double after soaking; for example, 125 g dried noodles will become 250 g when soaked.

china

China is the original source of noodles throughout Asia. They are served towards the end of a traditional Chinese meal, but in the West, people are happy to eat them any time.

Thin Yellow Wheat Noodles (egg, wheat flour)
Fresh: rinse in warm water and boil for 2 minutes.
Dried: boil about 5 minutes.

Thick Yellow Wheat Noodles (egg, wheat flour)
Fresh: rinse in warm water and boil for 3 minutes.
Dried: boil about 8 minutes.

Wheat Noodles (wheat flour)
Fresh: rinse in warm water and boil for 4 minutes.
Dried: boil about 5 minutes.

Rice Stick Noodles, Rice Vermicelli (rice flour)
Always dried: soak in hot water for 15 minutes and boil for 1 minute or deep-fry for 30 seconds.

Rice Ribbon Noodles – ho fun (rice flour)
When fresh, often sold in folded sheets, like a small book. Sometimes need to be cut into wide strips before use. Can be used for Vietnamese noodle soups (*pho*).
Fresh: rinse in hot water, then cook for 1 minute.
Dried: cook for 2–3 minutes.

Spring Roll Wrappers (wheat flour)
Always fresh, sold in refrigerated section: fill, then steam for 5 minutes, or deep-fry 1 minute.

Gyoza Wrappers (egg, wheat flour)
Always fresh, sold in refrigerated section: boil, steam or fry 5–7 minutes or deep-fry 1 minute.

Wonton Wrappers (egg, wheat flour)
Always fresh, sold in refrigerated section: boil 4–5 minutes, with stuffing, or deep-fry 1 minute.

Beanthread or Cellophane Noodles (mung bean starch)
Always dried: soften in boiling water 15 minutes and boil for 1 minute or deep-fry for 30 seconds.

Shanghai Noodles (wheat, or wheat and egg)
Fresh: round, fresh egg noodles, rinse in warm water, then boil for 1–2 minutes until tender.
Dried: white dried wheat-flour noodles, similar to Japanese somen. Cook as for somen.

korea

Tangmyon Noodles (sweet potato and mung bean starch) Can be difficult to find, but sometimes in specialist markets. Brownish-grey in colour and very translucent.
Always dried: soften in boiling water for 10 minutes, then stir-fry for up to 1 minute.

Naengmyon Noodles (buckwheat flour)
Always dried: soften in boiling water for 10 minutes, then stir-fry up to 1 minute.

japan

All dried Japanese noodles should be cooked in the same way. Bring a saucepan of water to the boil, add the noodles and return to the boil. Skim with a slotted spoon, then add a splash of cold water, return to the boil, then skim again. Repeat 2–3 times. When cooked, rinse to remove excess starch and reheat by dipping in boiling water.

Soba Noodles (buckwheat flour)
Fresh: rinse in warm water and boil for 1 minute.
Dried: boil for 5–6 minutes.
Also available: green cha-soba noodles (buckwheat flour and green tea).

Udon Noodles (wheat flour)
Fresh: rinse in warm water and boil for 2 minutes.
Dried: boil for about 10 minutes.

Ramen Noodles (egg and wheat flour)
Fresh: rinse in warm water and boil for 2 minutes.
Dried: boil for about 5 minutes.

Somen Noodles (wheat flour)*
Fresh: rinse in warm water and boil for 2 minutes.
Dried: boil for about 3 minutes.
Also available: pink shiso somen (flavoured with shiso leaves), green cha somen (flavoured with green tea).

Harusame or 'Spring Rain' Noodles (dried hair-thin filaments of rice flour, sometimes potato or tapioca flour)
Always dried: soften in hot water for 15 minutes, then serve as they are or reheat.

Shirataki 'White Waterfall' or 'Snowed Black Bean Curd' Noodles (starch of the devil's tongue plant, related to sweet potatoes)
Always fresh: rinse in warm water, then add to a dish: they soften in contact with the sauce.

thailand

Noodle dishes were introduced to Thailand from China, and they are the only foods eaten with chopsticks. Other foods are eaten with the fingers, fork and/or spoon.

Broad flat rice noodles – sen yai (rice flour)
Also known as rice stick or rice river noodles.
Fresh: rinse in hot water and boil for 1 minute.
Dried: soften in hot water for 15 minutes, then boil for 2–3 minutes.

Thin egg and rice flour noodles – ba mee (egg and rice flour) Sold in skeins.
Always fresh: rinse in warm water and boil for 3–4 minutes.

Thin rice stick vermicelli noodles – sen mee (rice flour)
Usually dried: soak in hot water for 15 minutes, then boil or stir-fry 1 minute.

Flat rice sticks – sen lek, jantaboon (rice flour)
Usually dried: soften in hot water for 15 minutes, then boil for 45 seconds.

Beanthread, Cellophane or Glass Noodles – wun sen (mung bean flour)
Very thin, transparent vermicelli.
Usually dried: soak in hot water for 15 minutes and boil or deep-fry for 1 minute.

vietnam

Most Vietnamese noodles are made from rice flour or mung beans. They can be eaten at any time of the day, alone or with other dishes.

Fine ricestick vermicelli noodles – *banh hoi* (rice flour)
Always dried: soak in hot water for 5 minutes, then steam for 5 minutes.

Thin rice vermicelli noodles – *bun* (rice flour)
Used in soups and spring rolls.
Always dried: boil for 1–2 minutes.

Wide ricestick noodles – *banh pho* (rice flour)
Wide rice stick noodles, also known as soup noodles, used in *pho bo* and *pho ca*.
Fresh: rinse in hot water before using.
Dried: soak 5 minutes in hot water, to rehydrate, then boil for 1–2 minutes. Can also be stir-fried deep-fried. Used whole or cut into quarters.

Ricepaper wrappers – *banh trang* (rice flour)
Dried ricepaper sheets, used for spring rolls.
Always dried: dip in hot water for 30 seconds to soften, then add fillings, roll up and serve, or deep-fry.

Beanthread, glass or cellophane noodles (mung bean flour)
Regarded as a vegetable in Vietnam. Used a filling for spring rolls. Firm squeaky bite. Good for those on gluten-free diets.
Dried: soak in hot water for 15 minutes.

philippines

Miswa Noodles (wheat flour)
Similar to Japanese somen noodles.
Always dried: cook in simmering water until tender, then use in soups or stir-fries.

Lumpia Wrappers (see Spring Roll Wrappers)

malaysia and singapore

One of the most famous cooking styles in Malaysia and Singapore is Straits Chinese Nonya cooking, a mixture of Chinese and Malay traditions.

Laksa Noodles (rice flour)
Local name for rice vermicelli, used in spicy noodle laksas or soups. Prepare as for Chinese rice vermicelli.

the basics: asian stocks

In East and South-east Asia, a wide range of stocks is used to add flavour, or even as the main ingredient in curries and soups, especially light soups with quick-cooking seafood, vegetables or noodles. Flavour and clarity are prized – in the first recipe, you will find an excellent technique for clarifying stock.

first dashi stock

Dashi stock powder is convenient, but it's easy to make your own.

1 sheet kombu, toasted over a gas flame for a few seconds or under a grill for 30 seconds

25 g grated dried bonito

Makes about 1 litre

Put the kombu into a saucepan with 1 litre cold water. Bring it slowly to the boil over gentle heat. Just before boiling, remove the kombu. Stir in the bonito, turn off the heat and let cool. When the bonito has settled to the bottom, skim off any foam with a slotted spoon, then ladle the stock through a strainer and use.

Second Dashi The kombu and bonito can be used to make a second batch. The stock will keep in the refrigerator for 3 days, or can be frozen.

asian chicken stock

A delicious chicken stock of good quality – fat free and very clear.

1 kg chicken carcasses, wings, or wingtips

5 cm fresh ginger, peeled and sliced

250 g shallots or large-bulbed spring onions

8 garlic cloves, lightly crushed

10 peppercorns

6 fresh coriander stalks with leaves

Makes about 1.5 litres

Remove and discard all fat from the carcasses and chop roughly. Put into a large saucepan and add 3 litres of cold water. Heat to simmering point, but do not let boil. Using a slotted spoon, skim off any foam that rises to the surface. Add the remaining ingredients, then heat to simmering point, letting the surface break with slow bubbles in several places to release the steam.

Simmer for about 2½ hours. Drain off the liquid – which should be clear – through a muslin-lined sieve into a bowl. Let cool, then freeze until the fat has congealed on the top.

Scrape off the fat and discard. While the liquid is frozen, tilt the bowl and pour a little boiling water over the top to wash off any remaining fat. Transfer the stock to a clean pan, bring to a rolling boil and reduce to 1.5 litres. Use immediately or freeze in convenient quantities.

thai-style stock

This simple stock can be made with all chicken or a combination of chicken and pork. Use it as a basis for soups and curries.

about 1.5 kg chicken carcasses, chopped into 4–6 pieces, or wings

about 500 g lean pork with bones, cut into large chunks

1 handful of fresh coriander, with stalks and roots if possible

a large pinch of salt

Makes about 1 litre

Put the chicken, pork and coriander into a large saucepan, then add the salt and about 2 litres water. Bring to the boil and, using a slotted spoon, skim off any foam that rises to the surface. Repeat the skimming several times, then reduce the heat to a gentle simmer and cook for about 1 hour.

Remove from the heat and let cool. When cool, pour gently through a fine sieve, so as not to disturb too much of the sediment. Discard the bones and sediment.

Chill, preferably overnight, in the refrigerator, then scrape off the fat from the top of the stock. Use immediately or freeze in convenient quantities.

south-east asian chicken or pork stock

A basic stock made from any available poultry or meat. The sugar-salt-spice combination is common in Vietnam.

2 kg chicken carcasses or pork bones, or a combination of both

3 cm fresh ginger, peeled and sliced

1 shallot or onion, cut into wedges

a large pinch of salt

a pinch of sugar

Makes about 1.5 litres

Put the bones into a large saucepan and pour over enough cold water to cover. Bring slowly to the boil, then boil for 10–15 minutes. Using a slotted spoon, skim off any foam that rises to the surface. Repeat skimming several times.

Reduce the heat, add the ginger, shallot or onion, salt and sugar, then simmer for about 2 hours.

Strain through a fine sieve, discarding the bones, flavourings and sediment. Chill in the refrigerator, remove the fat and use immediately or freeze in convenient quantities.

vietnamese beef stock

This is the basis of the legendary Vietnamese beef noodle soup, *pho bo*, as well as other soups.

1 kg shin of beef, with bones, cut into 3 cm slices

500 g stewing beef, in the piece

3 cm fresh ginger, peeled and sliced

a pinch of salt

3 tablespoons fish sauce, such as *nam pla*

2 whole star anise

1 cinnamon stick, broken

2 onions, sliced

Makes about 1 litre

Put the bones into a large saucepan and pour over enough cold water to cover. Bring to the boil and boil for 15 minutes. Using a slotted spoon, skim off any foam that rises to the surface. When the foam stops rising, reduce the heat, add the beef and simmer for about 2 hours.

Add the ginger, salt, fish sauce, star anise, cinnamon stick and onions and simmer for 30 minutes.

Strain through a fine sieve, discarding the bones, flavourings and sediment. Set aside the meat for another dish. Chill in the refrigerator, then remove the fat. Use the stock within 3 days or freeze in convenient quantities.

index

acknowledgements

recipes

photography

Sonia Stevenson
Malay chicken soup, Monks' vegetables, Green Thai fish curry, Braised duck and ginger, Red-cooked pork, Asian chicken stock, Thai-style stock, South-east Asian chicken or pork stock, Vietnamese beef stock.

Clare Ferguson
Bulgogi, Chinese dim sum, Chinese crispy deep-fried wontons, Indonesian chicken martabak, Chinese crab and sweetcorn soup, Spicy Thai chicken soup, Tempura, Chinese fried rice, Korean oyster pancakes, Bangkok chicken, Stir-fried chicken with greens, Hunan chicken, Japanese salt-grilled chicken, Peking duck, Deep-fried chilli beef, Chinese toffee apples, The basics: rice.

Fiona Smith
Bok choy rolls, Chopstick chicken wontons, Little Szechuan chicken steamed buns, Plum sauce, Sweet and sour sesame sauce, Soy and ginger sauce, Sweet chilli sauce, Sweet and sour pickled vegetables, Orange and almond fortune cookies, Five-spice custard tarts.

Elsa Petersen-Schepelern
Vietnamese pork balls, Thai crabcakes, Vietnamese spring rolls, Sushi, Sushi allsorts, Thai condiments, Indonesian gado-gado, Thai spicy prawn salad, Thai noodle salad, Vietnamese salad wraps, Vietnamese chicken salad, Japanese soba noodle salad, Chinese treasure soup, Vietnamese watercress soup, Singapore laksa, Japanese fresh corn soup, Chinese mushrooms, Stir-fried water chestnuts and sprouts, Vietnamese stir-fried bok choy, Pattypan snake beans in spicy coconut milk, Vietnamese pancakes, Japanese steamed fish, Malaysia Penang tamarind fish laksa, Otak otak, Chinese steamed fish, Crisp Thai noodles, Singapore pork satays, Indonesian beef satays, Sticky rice with mango, Black rice with red fruits, Watermelon and lime smoothie, Mango and coconut milk, The basics: noodles, Dashi.

Peter Cassidy
Pages 2–3, 4–5, 6–7, 17, 18, 21–23, 25, 26, 29, 30, 35, 39 above left, 70, 84, 88 below left, above left and right,100–101, 104, 107, 113–115,117, 118, 121, 122, 124, 138.

Peter Cassidy
Pages 8, 16, 22, 26, 30–31, 32–33, 34, 41, 42, 46, 49, 63, 80, 100, 102–103, 104, 106, 109.

William Lingwood
Pages 1, 2, 4–5, 6, 7, 11, 12, 14–15, 28, 36–37, 61, 66, 77, 78–79, 84–85, 92, 95, 96–97, 113, 115, 118, 119, 122–123, 126–127, 129, 130–131, 132–133, 135, 136–137.

Jeremy Hopley
Pages 3, 19, 21, 25, 38, 45, 51, 52, 55, 57, 58, 64, 69, 70, 73, 75, 82, 86, 89, 90, 99, 110, 116, 125.

Ian Wallace
Page 120.

Simon Wheeler
Page 139.

Recipes in this book were previously published in other Ryland Peters & Small cookbooks including *Casseroles: from Tagine to Coq au Vin* by Sonia Stevenson; *Chicken: from Maryland to Kiev, Rice: from Risotto to Sushi, Streetfood* and *The Flavours of China* by Clare Ferguson; *Dim Sum* by Fiona Smith; *Juices and Tonics, Wok: Dishes from China, Japan and South-east Asia, Salads, Grill Pan Cooking* and *Blended Soups* by Elsa Petersen-Schepelern.